CONTENTS

About the Author

Dee Pilgrim completed the pre-entry, periodical journalism course at the London College of Printing before working on a variety of music and women's titles. As a freelancer and full-time member of staff she has written numerous articles and interviews for *Company*, *Cosmopolitan*, *New Woman*, *Woman's Journal* and *Weight Watchers* magazines. For many years she covered new output by singer/songwriters for *Top* magazine, which was distributed via Tower Records stores, and during this period interviewed the likes of Tori Amos, Tom Robinson and Joan Armatrading. As a freelancer for Independent Magazines she concentrated on celebrity interviews and film, theatre and restaurant reviews for magazines such as *Ms London*, *Girl About Town*, *LAM* and *Nine To Five*, and in her capacity as a critic she has appeared on both radio and television. She is currently the film reviewer for *Now* magazine. When not attending film screenings she is active within the Critics' Circle and is on the committee for their annual film awards event. Dee is a published songwriter and is currently engaged in writing the narrative to an as yet unpublished trilogy of children's illustrated books.

Acknowledgements

Many thanks to the people who agreed to be interviewed for this book and for the many useful insights they gave me into the performing arts as a profession. I would especially like to thank Tania Peach for arranging for me to visit Mountview Academy and would also like to thank the members of the Critics' Circle who offered extremely useful contacts. Ian Bramley at Dance UK and Harriet Wigginton at the Council for Dance Education and Training (CDET) were both extremely helpful, as was Nicole Hay of the National Council for Drama Training (NCDT) who provided me with course information. Kelly Wiffen at Equity provided the figures for Equity minimum wage rates. I would also like to thank the National Music Council (NMC) for the use of facts and figures from its 2002 'Counting The Notes' report. Pippa Rimmer at Futureshots gave me a fascinating insight into the rise of the short-film format. Many thanks to the Society of London Theatre for the use of information from its 1999 'After Wyndham (key issues in London theatre)' report (written by Tony Travers of the London School of Economics). Finally, a huge thank you to Carlton Edwards, my songwriting partner in crime.

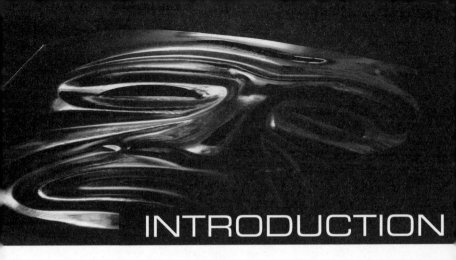

What's the Story, Morning Glory?

So, you want to be in films? You want to make it big on *X Factor*, or maybe even dance all night on *Strictly Come Dancing*? You want to smell the greasepaint and stand in the spotlights while an adoring audience hangs on your every word? Well, then you'll be joining a very large club because these days everybody seems to want to be a performer.

It's really no surprise the performing arts are such a popular career choice because for those actors, musicians and dancers who do last in the business the rewards – both personal and financial – can be huge. There are the critically acclaimed films, albums and dance pieces, a public that loves you, a large salary, and the glamorous lifestyle celebrity can bring. But there is also the downside, the constant pressure of being in the public eye, the uncertainty if it will all last, then the times when you have a flop, when your agent stops ringing, and the public doesn't seem to love you any more. And this is what you have to look forward to if you actually make it – the sad fact is that most never even get that far.

THE FAME GAME

Andy Warhol once said that everybody will be famous for 15 minutes. For some 15 minutes is all they ever get, for others it is more like 15 seconds. For every actress that wins an award there are a thousand still waiting on tables, temping in offices, and longing for their big break. For every Scissor Sisters there are a dozen would-be bands sitting in dingy rehearsal studios waiting to be discovered, and for every ballerina like Darcey Bussell there is a flock of dying swans. This is a tough business, a profession that takes no prisoners, a career where you are ultimately your own product and must keep selling yourself each and every day. This is no place for shrinking violets.

GETTING IN THE KNOW

But if you've picked up this book it means you are interested in learning more about the performing arts. You want the real story on what it's all about, what you should expect, and what you can actually do in the business. You want to know what makes performing such a pleasure and joy, but also what makes it such a pain. You want to find out what people in the industry already have experienced, how and where they trained, and where their careers are going. Finally, you want to know what qualifications you will need to pursue your dream of becoming an actor or actress, musician or dancer. *Performing Arts Uncovered* is an honest appraisal of the industry, and what you can realistically achieve within it. It has to be because there is no use coming into this business with false illusions; there are already too many failed performers out there.

'You need to have a sense of humour and you need flexibility, humility and determination to make it in this industry.'

Kate Gielgud, actress/voice coach

THE RIGHT DIRECTION

For the purposes of this book we will be looking at the three main sections of the performing arts: drama, music and dance. You will find the main body of the book itself has been split into these three categories for ease of use. Deciding where jobs in the performing arts actually begin and end is a bit like asking how long is a piece of string. Basically, the string goes on as long as you are prepared to unravel it. This is because the industry is so very vast, generating billions of pounds in revenue and employing thousands of people in hundreds of different positions (everything from ticket-office staff to international stars). Instead of trying to cover every job, this book concentrates on those individuals closest to the performance process itself, i.e. the actors, musicians and dancers, although other, related jobs are also included and their roles explained. This means if you decide that performing is not for you, you may well find mentioned here some other position within the industry that suits you better.

THE SHOW MUST GO ON

The advent of new technology – increasing satellite and cable channels, DVD, Mini Disc, the iPod and mobile telephone wizardry – means the whole world now really *is* a stage and that in turn means we need more performers than ever before out there strutting their stuff.

'I think we are on the edge of something huge at the moment, it's really exciting,' says Pippa Rimmer of innovative company Futureshorts, set up in 2003 to promote and distribute short films. 'There are so many new platforms out there; there's video content on mobiles; you can download via the internet; we supply content to Sony Playstations; you get on a bus on the way home and they have screens, and now even Tube stations have screens. So many companies want to get their hands on really interesting content and that's not just adverts.'

This book will help you decide whether you could be part of this exciting new world of performance. In the theatre they say 'break a leg' when they want to wish an actor luck. However, luck is a difficult commodity to come by. Much better to read this book, know the low-down, be prepared and go into the industry with your eyes wide open, then the luck takes care of itself.

'When you're an actor, there's nothing better than working with other actors, rather than sitting at home alone waiting for the phone to ring.'

Kate Gielgud, actress/voice coach

FASCINATING FACT

A six minute video entitled *Evolution of Dance* has become the most viewed video of all time on the youtube website, having been seen more than 33.5 million times. Created by Judson Laipply the video shows him dancing his way through 32 songs. The video has now made him famous and led to corporate gigs for the likes of Hilton Hotels and American Airlines.

Source: Reuters

JARGON BUSTERS
CHAIR
In theatre, each different musician has a different 'chair' within the musicians' 'pit' (see opposite). So, if there are three keyboard players, their three different chairs are called Keyboards 1, Keyboards 2 and Keyboards 3. In London's West End once you have a specific chair then the chair is yours for life unless you do something terribly wrong. 'For life' can mean as long as the show lasts or for as long as you want the job. Some musicians have had their chairs on *Les Miserables* since it opened over 21 years ago.

CORPSING
When an actor or actress cannot keep a straight face and bursts into fits of giggles mid-performance they are said to have 'corpsed'. Nicholas Lyndhurst who plays Rodney in *Only Fools And Horses* is a serial corpser, as anyone who has seen his out-takes on *It'll Be Alright On The Night* will know.

DIGS
The affectionate term for the boarding houses, bed and breakfast, or other cheap, rented accommodation actors

still use while on tour. Spotlight's excellent *Contacts* book contains a Good Digs Guide (see Resources).

DRYING
'Drying' is when an actress or actor forgets their lines mid-performance (as in they have 'dried up'). If they do so on stage you may hear them say 'prompt' (see below).

FRONT OF HOUSE
At one time, theatres were known as 'playhouses', which is why to this day backstage staff may ask if such-and-such an actor is 'in the house' (i.e. is he actually on the premises). Front of house refers to exactly that, the part of the theatre that is in front of the stage and backstage areas and includes the box office, foyers, bars and auditorium. Front of house staff include ticket sellers, ushers, theatre managers and bar staff.

GIG
Although the word 'gig' is normally associated with the music world, actors use it as well. It basically means a job, so Coldplay may talk about doing a 'gig' at Brixton Academy, while to an actor a 'gig' may be work on an advert or a stint on tour.

THE PIT
The orchestra pit in a theatre. At classical concerts the orchestra is normally on stage in open view of the audience, but in ballet performances and in musical theatre the musicians are usually hidden from view in the pit.

PROMPT
The prompter, or better known as the prompt, sits out of sight of the audience in a theatre reading the written play or script as the actors perform it. If an actor forgets their lines, the prompt will then assist them by reading out the next few words of the script in order to jog their memory.

REPERTORY COMPANY
A theatre group that specialises in limited runs of a series of plays or pieces they have in their repertoire (hence the name) rather than on long runs of the same play. The repertory company is now something of a rarity.

RESTING
The polite term used when actors are out of work.

THE RIDER
A term dear to the hearts of rock bands everywhere. The rider is the provisions the concert promoter agrees to leave for the band in the backstage area. This will mostly consist of both soft and alcoholic drinks as well as some form of food. Certain major stars are so fussy about their rider they get very upset if it does not tally with what is stipulated in their contract. One very well-known star is rumoured to have had a major tantrum when she discovered her rider contained the wrong-coloured jelly babies!

ROADIES
The real term for roadies is 'road crew'. They are an important part of any live tour, be it theatrical, dance or music. They are responsible for taking down all the stage rigging, including mikes, lighting, special effects and amplifiers, packing them up and then transporting them (quite often right through the night and across country borders) on to the next venue on the tour. For a rock band such as Pink Floyd, renowned for its spectacular live shows, the road crew can employ substantial amounts of people. At present roadies are not unionised but in 2004 an initiative by the GMB union, Britain's general trade union, was started to explain the benefits union membership can bring (including access to pension plans and legal advice).

SHOWREEL
A showreel is like an audio/visual CV. Actors, dancers and musicians will edit down highlights of their performances onto a video and present this during casting calls or at

auditions. It gives the casting agent or show's director and producer an indication of what each candidate is capable of. Showreels should look professional and so can be expensive to produce but remember: you are your own product and you deserve to get the best marketing money can buy. For many budding film-makers – directors, producers, technicians – the short-film format is their favoured form of showreel. As Pippa Rimmer of Futureshorts explains: 'Shorts are perfect because they give you the chance to have an intensity and overall awareness of a director's vision and they are so much cheaper to make than feature films.'

TECHIES

The affectionate term for technical staff or technicians. The techies handle all the technical stuff such as lighting, rigging, sound, scenery, special effects, etc. Without them most modern-day theatrical performances, concerts, TV shows and films could not be produced.

FASCINATING FACT

In October 2006 *Les Miserables* celebrated a record-breaking 21 year run in the West End. Former stars of the show, including Michael Ball and Frances Ruffelle, joined the cast on stage for a special performance. The show has now been seen by 54 million people in 38 countries.

'If you are coming into this industry because you "want to be famous", then, in my opinion, you are likely to be disappointed at some stage along the line, even if you succeed.'

Jonathan Goodwin, professional magician, five tv's *Monkey Magic*

FASCINATING FACT

The Universal Music Group is the biggest music group in the world. Its artists include Eminem, Daniel Beddingfield and Jamie Cullum.

A NICE DAY AT THE OFFICE

Unless you are working in a secretarial or administration position within the performing arts you probably won't be located in an office. It's far more likely you will be in a rehearsal room, on stage in a theatre or concert hall, on a sound stage at a film or TV studio, in a recording studio, or on location. What you do at all these different places will depend on whether you are involved in drama, music or dance. See the chart opposite for just some of the different sites you could be working at in the performing arts – and some of the many different projects you could be working on.

JOBS IN PERFORMING ARTS

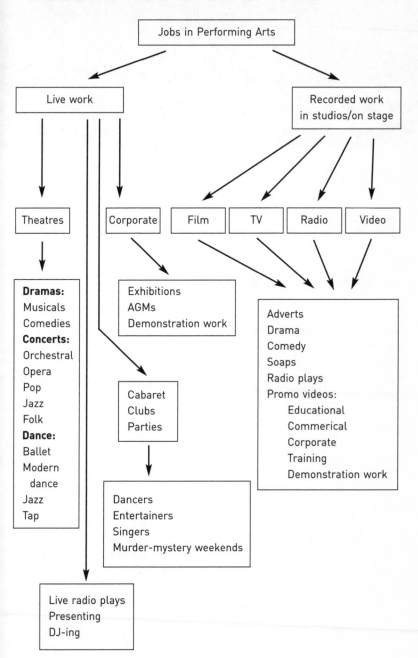

CHAPTER 1

Lights, Camera, Action!

DRAMA UNCOVERED

Once upon a time actors knew their place; it was on the stage where they plied their trade. These days they are everywhere; the proliferation of new media means the world of acting impinges on our real-life world on a day-to-day basis. Turn on your radio and there's *The Archers*, the long-running tale of life down on the farm and in the village of Ambridge. Radio is the medium where many new writers get their first break. For example, *Little Britain* was a radio programme before it hit our TV screens.

WHERE DO ACTORS WORK?

On TV, actors pop up in soaps, serious dramas, light comedies and you can't even avoid them during the ad breaks – chances are that the person extolling the virtues of a certain brand of toilet paper is an actor, too. At least if you go to the cinema or theatre you are making a positive choice to see actors at work, but what about at a corporate event, a murder-mystery weekend break or even at a children's party? If you decide to watch a dedicated music channel like MTV actors even turn up in the videos – you simply can't avoid them, especially in a world where new satellite and cable channels are hungry for drama programmes to fill their schedules. There has even been an interactive 'film' on the web called *Running Time* where viewers could watch a five minute episode and then choose one of three options as to what would happen to the actors in the next instalment.

WHAT OPPORTUNITIES ARE THERE?

You don't necessarily have to have had formal training to become an actor – temperament and character have as much to do with working in the industry as any qualifications you may or may not have. However, these days it really does help to have some sort of training as well as experience. This is because it will give you the skills to succeed and mark you out as a professional. But competition for places on accredited courses is extremely fierce – according to the National Council for Drama Training (NCDT) only between two and ten per cent of all students who apply for a place at drama school actually get onto an accredited course. Once you have completed an accredited course you will be eligible for full membership of the British actors' union, Equity, which means you will have a much better chance of getting professional jobs. According to the Office of National Statistics (ONS) 37,995 people stated their occupation as actor or performer in 2006. That's a lot of people acting up and down the country. The story doesn't end there either. Behind every actor is a small army of people who are just as essential for getting a production – be it on stage, radio or screen – ready and rolling. There are the writers, directors and producers, the voice coaches, costume designers and managers. Most importantly, there is the backstage staff such as the lighting and sound technicians, the riggers and prop-buyers. Then there are the people you might not even think about but who still have their part to play, such as ticket sales agents, theatre and cinema managers and ushers, theatrical agents and even film company lawyers.

In this book we will be concentrating most on actual performers and those people who have the roles closest to them. Take a look at the chart on the next page. Although it is not totally comprehensive, it will give you some indication of the vast wealth of careers you could pursue in the acting branch of the performing arts profession.

FASCINATING FACT

Drama is the eighth most popular degree to take at university after Business Management, Computer Science, Law, Design Studies, Psychology, English Literature and Medicine.
Source: UCAS

JOBS IN DRAMA

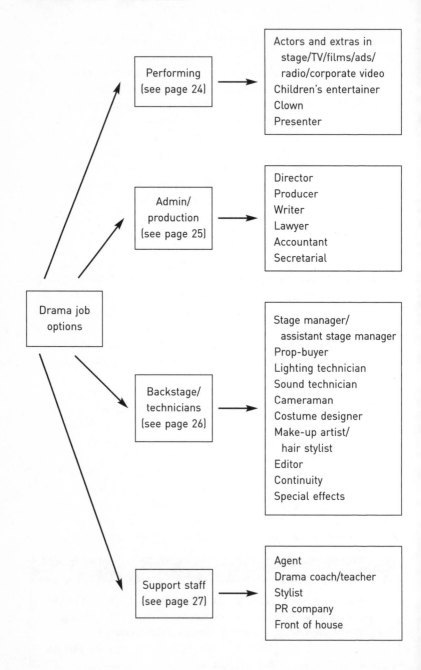

Performing
(see page 24)

→

Actors and extras in
  stage/TV/films/ads/
  radio/corporate video
Children's entertainer
Clown
Presenter

**Admin/
production**
(see page 25)

→

Director
Producer
Writer
Lawyer
Accountant
Secretarial

**Drama job
options**

**Backstage/
technicians**
(see page 26)

→

Stage manager/
  assistant stage manager
Prop-buyer
Lighting technician
Sound technician
Cameraman
Costume designer
Make-up artist/
  hair stylist
Editor
Continuity
Special effects

Support staff
(see page 27)

→

Agent
Drama coach/teacher
Stylist
PR company
Front of house

SPOTLIGHT ON SPOTLIGHT

Spotlight was founded in 1927 to provide casting information to the entertainment industry. For 80 years portraits and profiles of actors and actresses have appeared in Spotlight and casting directors have searched this unique database to find the perfect artist for the part. Getting into Spotlight will enhance your profile considerably – in fact, some actors consider it essential.

- Spotlight now has over 30,000 artists on its books.

- The Spotlight interactive website receives over 10 million page impressions a year.

- Every month, over 10,000 artists are put forward for over 700 roles via the Spotlight link.

- Spotlight publishes the invaluable annual *Contacts* book that lists everything from agents to film and TV distributors, and opera companies to set construction.

Source: Spotlight, www.spotlightcd.com
(For more information see Resources.)

CHAPTER 2

A Life Less Ordinary

THE DOWNSIDE

If your idea of the ideal job is well paid and secure with 9am to 5pm hours and at least four weeks' paid holiday a year, then you can rule out being an actor straightaway. There are some big downsides to this profession, as any actor worth his or her salt will tell you.

INSECURITY
According to Equity, the actors' and performers' trade union (see Resources), which has roughly 36,000 members, an average member may only work 12.4 weeks of the year. Obviously, if you are in a long-running TV series or theatre production, you will be guaranteed more work than this, but at any one time it is estimated only a third of actors in this country are actually working. This means for many jobbing actors performing is a hand-to-mouth existence where they must constantly hustle for work, send off their CVs, attend auditions and keep up with contacts. This can cause financial insecurity (see opposite). Even worse, constant rejection, when you keep going up for jobs and not getting them, can cause distressing emotional insecurity, which in turn can affect an actor's performance. The way most actors deal with this is by having an alternative day job, and by keeping busy doing other things.

'When people are not ringing you up it really chips away at your self-esteem, so you need to go off and do other things like unpaid read-throughs of new plays, workshops, and voice work.'

Kate Gielgud, actress/voice coach

LOW PAY

If you think all actors live in flash houses and drive expensive cars, think again. Of course, the big stars are well recompensed for their work, but most actors only earn modest wages throughout their careers. While people like Billy Connolly may have now joined the $1 million-a-film club (he was rumoured to earn this for his appearance in *The Last Samurai*), Equity members can earn as little as £300 a week. This is why it is so important to have another skill that can earn you money while you are 'resting', such as secretarial or IT skills. We will explore the financial aspects of acting more in Chapter 3.

ANTISOCIAL HOURS

If you like going out in the evenings and having weekends free to spend with friends then live theatre work really won't suit you. Your weekday evenings will be spent performing and most Saturdays will consist of two performances (the matinee and evening performances). Even if you become a regular on a TV soap the hours will be very long because you have to cram in so much filming every day. This is especially true during the shooting of a film where your make-up call can come at 4am, while the last scene of the day may not be shot until after 10pm. The schedule becomes even more frantic if you are shooting on location and have to wait for bad weather to pass. (If you want to see just how bad shooting on location can get, watch *Lost In La Mancha*, the documentary of director Terry Gilliam's disastrous attempts to film *Don Quixote* with Johnny Depp on location in Spain.)

FASCINATING FACT

Between 2004 and 2006 London's film industry grew by almost a third, making it the world's third biggest centre for film-making after Hollywood and New York. Apparently

> **an average of 35 shoots took place every day in 2005 and a day's filming in the capital is worth up to £450,000 to London's economy in terms of wages, taxes, food and parking fees.**
>
> **Source: *London Evening Standard***

ACTING UP

If there are so many downsides to this profession, why do people want to do it in the first place? The answer is simple: people become actors and actresses because they *love* performing. It gives them a legitimate excuse to play to an audience, and to be the centre of attention. For most it is a vocation, not a calculated career move. Some are more suited to the profession than others, which will mainly come down to natural-born talent, however, there are other personal and physical factors that will help you to be a success in the acting world.

STAMINA

Acting is not for the faint of heart or the weak of body. The hours are long, the work can be physically demanding and the pressures – and most especially the performances – can be emotionally draining. You have to look after yourself. This is especially true of young women in the profession who sometimes feel under pressure to be very thin and to watch their diet. Many actors now take courses such as yoga, Pilates and meditation to ensure they keep their bodies and minds in tip-top shape.

ABILITY TO WORK IN A TEAM

Unless you are putting on a one-man play, most theatrical, TV or film performances are collaborative efforts. There may be a great many other actors performing with you, then there's the director, maybe the writer, the stage manager and all the backstage staff to consider. You will have to interact with all these other people and so being a team-player is essential. In fact, one aspect of the profession many people love is the great feeling of camaraderie that can build up between members of a cast and its crew, and the friendships that are made and can last a lifetime.

COMMUNICATION SKILLS

Think about what an actor actually does. He or she is conveying words and concepts written by a playwright or scriptwriter to an audience. You really do have to have a way with words and with physical gestures in order to make the message clear. You also need to understand directions given to you and to be able to make yourself understood. This is why a confident and clear voice is essential.

FLEXIBILITY

As you will have seen by now, an actor's life is anything other than ordinary. One week you could be doing a comedy cameo in panto in Blackpool, the next month doing a voiceover for a TV advert in London, and the month after that you could be playing a serious role on tour in Europe. If you can adapt to a career that is constantly changing and see it as an exciting challenge then acting could be for you.

TRANSFERABLE SKILLS

You'll also need to be flexible when 'resting'. If you read the case studies dotted throughout this book you will see that time and time again actors, dancers and musicians talk about the need to have other skills outside of their 'proper' job so they can earn money while not working. These jobs need to be short term or freelance so if a gig does come up suddenly you have the flexibility to be able to take it. For actors, ideal jobs include waiting on tables, working as bar staff, telesales, office work, teaching acting classes, or getting training to be a practitioner such as a voice coach, masseuse, or yoga, t'ai chi or Pilates instructor. Remember: in this profession you are guaranteed to have periods of unemployment (on any given day in 2005 two-thirds of Britain's actors were not employed acting), so you need to have another string to your bow so you can weather the financial bad times. In fact, seeing a gap in the market, actors Ben Hull and Anna Acton have set up Next Big Thing Recruitment, an agency tailored to employers seeking the services of actors between parts.

GOOD MEMORY

Actors have to memorise lines; it is a big part of their jobs, and often they will have a very short period in order to learn their parts (this is especially true on TV soaps where shooting is very fast). Having a good memory is therefore essential and it can also help where contacts are concerned. People tend to move around within the industry a lot and remembering their names, faces and where you know them from will stand you in good stead at auditions and open calls.

APPEARANCE

All the actors interviewed for this book agreed on one thing: an attractive appearance is one of your biggest assets in the modern industry. Nine times out of ten, if two equally talented actors go up for a job, the most attractive of the pair will get it. Actors such as Mackenzie Crook (*The Office*, *Pirates of the Caribbean*) have shown this is not always the case, and have made an asset out of having a face with strong character, but you should be aware that you might sometimes lose out on a job because of the way you look.

DETERMINATION

Whatever else you do in this industry, the one thing you can never do is give up. Keep on smiling, even when you haven't had a job for months, and keep sending out those CVs and going to those auditions. You have to be tenacious and optimistic because the only person who can really sell your talents is you. No actor ever made it by sitting in a corner lamenting their fate. Get out there, be seen, and shine!

ADD-ONS

One of the best ways to increase your worth as an actor or actress is to have add-on skills. These are the extra skills you can learn that may come in useful one day, the most basic being to have a clean driving licence (you never know, you might end up on a TV series driving an ambulance), while the more exotic skills include fire-eating, horse-riding, and the ability to play the piano or to swordfight. With the recent phenomenal rise in the popularity of musicals (see the box opposite), the ability to sing, or dance, but most preferably to do both, will really stand you in good stead. Many of the better drama schools teach certain add-ons as a matter of course, but it's never too late to learn a few off your own bat as well.

FASCINATING FACT

Last year, musicals overtook straight plays in the West End, in terms of both audience and revenue. The top ten musicals took advance bookings of at least £64.1 million, with *The Sound of Music* and *Billy Elliot* accounting for £25.1 million between them. In contrast, just six plays were running, mostly at only 70 to 80 per cent audience capacity, while musicals enjoyed over 90 per cent capacity.

Source: *London Evening Standard*

DON'T PUT YOUR DAUGHTER ON THE STAGE, MRS WORTHINGTON!

'Her personality
Is not in reality
Inviting enough,
Exciting enough
For this particular sphere.'

So wrote Noel Coward. Even if you have great natural talent as an actor, there are some personality traits and physical conditions that can hold you back. You may not suffer from any of them now, but it is good to know what they are, and to monitor yourself for them in the future.

READING DIFFICULTIES/DYSLEXIA

As we've already seen, learning lines is a big part of any actor's job. Therefore, if you find reading difficult, or suffer from dyslexia, this may not be the profession for you and you may find a backstage or support staff role better utilises other skills and talents you have.

CHRONIC SHYNESS

Isn't it funny how some of us can be veritable Nicole Kidmans in the safety of our own rooms but clam up completely when faced with an audience? Part of the art of being an actor is to lose 'oneself' and become your character while totally forgetting there is an audience out there. If you are terribly self-conscious you may find this impossible to do. You may have a profound love for drama but a job in the profession that does not entail actually performing may be more suitable.

INABILITY TO COPE WITH PERFORMANCE PRESSURE

Most of the actors interviewed for this book admitted to getting first-night nerves at some point in their careers. In fact, some actors get nerves every night, ranging from a tightness in the chest and butterflies in the tummy to full-on nausea. Performance pressure can come on at any time during the run of a show. Daniel Day-Lewis walked out halfway through a performance of *Hamlet* at the National Theatre when the pressure got too much for him. Different people learn to cope in their own ways but if you think this could seriously affect your physical health and your emotional well-being, you might like to consider a role out of the limelight.

LACK OF PATIENCE

If only 30 per cent of actors are working at any one time, that means 70 per cent of them are sitting at home twiddling their thumbs. Actually, they are not, they are busy earning their living by doing other things and know that they have to keep plugging away in the industry to get results. Their mantra becomes 'be patient'. If you can't bear the thought of 'resting' for the majority of the time you may find the frustration is just too much and you'd be better off getting out of acting altogether and pursuing a different career.

SUSCEPTIBILITY TO DEPRESSION

It is tough when you keep getting rejected, when that role you *know* you are more than capable of filling goes to someone else. When the phone doesn't ring and you don't get called for audition it can hurt like crazy. But actors have to have the ability to bounce right back and try again, and again. If you find yourself giving way to depression and despair you will not be able to sustain yourself through long periods of 'resting' and the renewed chance of getting rejected again when you do go for audition. Your mental well-being is more important than any part, however big, and if you know you have a tendency to become down-hearted and depressed you are going to have to seriously consider whether acting is for you.

'The best piece of advice I can give is to be true to yourself, and to know who you are. It is a very tough and competitive industry, and if you are armed with those two things, then you will be able to survive a lot longer than most.'

Jonathan Goodwin, professional magician, five TV's *Monkey Magic*

TANJA MCGHIE, 26, ACTRESS

'I'd wanted to go to drama school since I was about 10 years old but when I sat down and worked out how much they cost I realised I didn't have enough money to go to the likes of Central. I contemplated doing a degree at university but in the end I plumped for the Academy Drama School because it was geared up to let you work and earn as you learned. The course is called the full-time Acting Evening Course and you work during the day and then the minimum amount of hours of study you have to do is between 6.30pm and 10.30pm every day, Monday to Friday, and then all day on Saturday. I trained for two years and there were two showcases at the end of the course and about 20 agents came to each showcase.

'I didn't get an agent out of that but I did eventually get work doing children's theatre and a lot of pantomime – which was good as it pays quite well. Not having an agent is hard though, you have to be so motivated to actively go and look for work, you really have to rely on yourself. A lot of actors will tell you it is auditions that put them off, but for me the worst part is having to stay motivated all the time. Another hard thing is that the pay is so bad you really do have to do other work as well and it is hard to get back from a day's work and then sit at your computer writing off for acting jobs.

'I was only 19 years old when I started at drama school so I did bar work and I also worked as a tour guide which was great for my voice and self-confidence, but mostly I have done office work. It is still relatively easy to get general office work through temp agencies. The work may be dull but the pay is OK – you can get £9 an hour even if you don't have computer skills.

'Nothing I have ever done as a temp has ever made me as happy as when I am acting. I love the rehearsal period because the beginning of a run is always exciting. I'm quite proud to be in this profession so it always makes me feel happy and contented when I am in a production, no matter what it is. I'm just glad to be doing it. The problem is when you have to take really crappy day jobs because that can really make you despondent. But I certainly wouldn't consider giving up the acting. When you hit really low points you just have to remember how much effort you have put into it and try to remain positive. I just remember how great acting is when I'm actually doing it and I find that pulls me through.

'Apart from the lack of money or job security the thing I hate the most is the schmoozing you have to do to get jobs. It's not pleasant but in this business it really is a lot to do with who you know. Another thing is, I still get terrible nerves, it's bizarre but they seem to get worse the longer the run goes on. Stage fright is one of the worst downsides to the business because you would rather be doing anything, even queuing at Tesco, than to be up there on that stage.

'Realistically, in five years' time I would like to have found an enjoyable day job that makes me feel good about myself and still be doing three or four shows a year that pay at least Equity minimum. I don't think I'll ever be constantly employed as an actress but three or four shows a year would be fine.'

FASCINATING FACT

The London Eye has become the capital's top film location appearing in such diverse films and TV shows as *Stormbreaker*, *Hustle* and *The Apprentice*.

Source: *London Evening Standard*

CHAPTER 3

Drama Queens (and Kings)

So now you know a bit more about what skills you need to bring to the profession, but what could you actually do in the business? By now you may well have a very good idea about what an actor's job remit is, but the chart shown on page 12 may contain a few job titles with which you are unfamiliar. Here's the low-down on the jobs in the profession.

PERFORMING

This is it; this is what most people who enter the performing arts strive to be – the performer, the person who takes on the role written down for them on the page. Actors and actresses appear in plays on stage, TV, radio and film. One day they could be reciting Shakespeare or Brecht, the next appearing in a soap such as *EastEnders* or *Hollyoaks*. They could be utilising other skills such as their singing and dancing in a West End musical such as *Evita* or *Spamalot*, or they could be doing something else entirely, perhaps a voice-over for a car advertisement, or a roleplay (they pretend to be a patient or a customer while a doctor or trainee learns how to deal with them). There are other types of performers in the profession as well, such as mime artists, magicians, stunt men and presenters.

ADMINISTRATION/PRODUCTION

WRITING
Quite high up the 'food chain' in the world of drama is the playwright or scriptwriter (although many whinge that their contribution to the whole process is not appreciated enough). Without those words on the page the actors have nothing to work with – a bit like a potter with no clay. Some actors combine their performing role with that of the writer (Emma Thompson starred in *Sense and Sensibility* and also wrote the screen adaptation, while Richard O'Brien not only wrote *The Rocky Horror Show* but also starred in the stage and film versions). Many playwrights become household names, like Alan Bennett and David Hare and many also fill the dual roles of writer/director.

DIRECTING
It is the director's job to have an overall vision of what each theatrical piece will look and sound like when it is finally up there on the stage or screen. He or she will work closely with the actors to interpret the script to bring out its true meaning. A good director liaises with the set designer and lighting and sound crews so that the production looks and sounds as they want. Some actors become directors (Clint Eastwood or Kenneth Branagh who has just directed a film version of Mozart's opera *The Magic Flute*), and many people now study specifically to be directors at university and drama school. The director often works with an assistant director.

PRODUCTION
The role of producer or production manager may not sound very creative, but believe me, this is a job where you always have to flex those creative muscles! This is because producers are the money men and women: they have to work out just what everything is going to cost, make sure they have the finances in place to cover it and then bust a gut not to go over budget. This means they are coordinating all the different departments, making sure their work is finished on time so as not to accrue overtime bills. Some production managers work in-house, i.e. they are

employed by a particular theatre or theatre group, but most work freelance, especially in the film world where the producer's name is often as important as the director's (producer Jerry Bruckheimer's name can be seen on many big action films such as *Bad Boys* and *Top Gun*). Also attached to the production office are the administrators, accountants and secretarial staff, and usually on the team somewhere will be a lawyer, sorting out contractual problems, royalties and rights.

BACKSTAGE/TECHNICIANS

STAGE MANAGERS

One of the most important people backstage is the stage manager who acts as a communicator between the actors, the technical staff and any support crew who may also be involved. He or she is responsible for making sure the actors, musicians and dancers turn up to rehearsals and performances on time and know what they are doing, and that the props department, costumes, hair and make-up are also in the right place at the right time. This can be a logistical nightmare so anyone contemplating this role has to be able to take responsibility. They must have a logical, common-sense approach and not get panicked easily. On large shows with big casts the stage manager may employ the aid of an assistant stage manager or a deputy stage manager.

SETTING THE SCENE

The set designer and prop-buyer are the people responsible for the sometimes magical look of stage productions and films. If the director says he wants the action to be set within Aladdin's cave, they have to make sure that is what the director gets. Often they will be working under restrictions that will test their creativity to the full: at small theatre companies the budget may only be modest, or the stage area so cramped that the set design will have to be modified to accommodate the props and the cast. They must also take into account safety considerations: the one thing they don't want on opening night is for the cast to be falling over the scenery, but such glitches are normally smoothed out at technical rehearsals.

Also working on the visual aspects of a production, be it TV, film or theatre are the costume designer, wardrobe department and hair and make-up. While the wardrobe department is responsible for the actual production and upkeep of the costumes, the costume designer draws the initial designs, oversees them as they are being made and refines them during the dress rehearsal when any problems can be sorted out. Hair and make-up is also an integral part of a production's look – everything from afro wigs and hippy face paint (from the show *Hair!*) to animal whiskers and fur (*Cats*).

LIGHTING AND SOUND

The lighting technicians are also important to the look of a production. By choosing various colours, filters and different strengths of light they can alter the feel and mood of the stage considerably. A large show may have a lighting designer working with a team of electricians, and on a film or TV set there is usually a lighting cameraman and riggers to set the lights up, while in small theatre groups all the lighting may be the responsibility of just one person. They have to coordinate closely with the set designer and once again, health and safety are an important part of their job. New technology has greatly increased the scope of what lighting technicians can achieve, but it also means they must keep abreast of the latest developments, especially in computer software.

The same can be said of the sound technicians who do everything from making sure the cast's microphones are working properly, to adding on all those evocative noises (an owl hooting or waves crashing in the background) that can add so much to the atmosphere of a production. Again, new technology means many sounds can now be produced via computers.

Other backstage or technical jobs include special effects, continuity (most often in films and TV) and editor (again, mainly in film or TV).

SUPPORT STAFF

AGENTS

They say that behind every big star there stands a good agent. However, finding one is never easy. Many agents attend the special graduation productions put on by the main drama schools each year and if you are a very lucky graduate, you could get an agent there. Others find clients through recommendations. Most budding actors find they need a body of work behind them before they can get themselves an agent. So why get one at all? Because having the name of an agent on your CV will make you look professional and says you are taking your career seriously.

An agent is there to push you in the direction of good jobs and to steer you clear of anything dodgy. An agent should act as a mentor to you, advising you on the auditions you should be going to and to whom you should be talking. Unfortunately, it doesn't always work that way and many actors discover they actually generate more work themselves than they ever get through an agent. Agents earn their money by taking a percentage of the fee for every job they secure for you. This is usually around the 15 per cent mark.

'Never, ever, pay an agent to take you onto their books.'

Kate Gielgud, actress/voice coach

CASTING DIRECTORS

An agent is a good person to know, but not half as good as a casting director. On large productions the casting director is responsible for finding exactly the right actors for each of the roles available. This can be incredibly important when they are casting the lead roles because if they don't get it right, everyone is going to notice. Getting to know casting directors from auditions and read-throughs is good because even if you don't get one job, you may well come to mind when they are casting for another production. In some cases, agents will do deals with casting directors. If the agent has a big name actor who the casting director wants, the agent may negotiate so other actors on their books are considered for smaller roles in order for the casting director to secure the services of the star. In smaller theatre companies the director takes on the responsibility for casting.

FRONT OF HOUSE ROLES

While all the roles above involve people plying their trade behind the scenes, out in front of house the theatre manager is sorting out the box office staff, the ushers and the bar staff. Their contributions are all important because they come into direct contact with the public and if you want people to come back again and again you must ensure their evening out is a pleasant experience, with efficient, polite staff making sure everything goes smoothly.

RELATED ROLES

Other jobs you may not have thought of are drama teacher, drama coach or voice coach, or doing the publicity for a show by working in the press office, or what about becoming a drama therapist or even a film or theatre critic?

FASCINATING FACT

Westminster Council has approved plans for producer Cameron Mackintosh to build a new 500 seat auditorium at the Queen's Theatre, Shaftesbury Avenue. A new flexible theatre called the Sondheim will open giving the Queen's 10 per cent more seating than the National Theatre on the South Bank.

Source: *West End Extra*

SHOW ME THE MONEY

HOW MUCH WILL YOU EARN?

For every megastar actor out there like Tom Cruise earning millions of dollars per film there are dozens of others scraping a living together. The one thing you don't come into the business for is to get rich. If you really want to know how bad it can get, read these sobering figures provided by Equity. In 2005, 90 per cent of Equity members earned less than £20,000, and 60 per cent earned less than £5,000. The following case study shows even an actor of many years' experience can find himself doing panto for the princely sum of just £300 a week. Obviously, some jobs pay more than others and if you are doing an advertisement or TV show or series where you get repeat fees the money can really add up over time. Equity has set its own minimum wages for its members. Of these, the lowest are obviously for work with small theatre companies, while one of the highest is for working with the BBC. At present the Equity minimum for eight performances (evening shows plus matinees) as an actor in the West End is

£366.82 a week and if you are working in a small-scale theatre the minimum is £300 a week. Stage managers have a minimum of £330. Directors get paid an upfront fee and then a weekly fee. In the West End the amounts are £2,339 upfront and then a weekly fee of £175.43. Remember, these are only minimum guidelines; if you are a named star, guaranteed to pull in the crowds, your agent or manager will be able to negotiate your fee. Yet even huge stars such as Nicole Kidman and Gwyneth Paltrow agreed to be paid the Equity norm when they both appeared on the West End stage.

ANDY SPIEGEL, ACTOR/CASTING DIRECTOR

Andy did a Performing Arts degree at Middlesex University with drama as his major and music and dance as his minors. He has worked pretty consistently ever since. He has appeared in many productions at the Nuffield Theatre in Southampton, including last year's production of *The School for Wives* by Molière; he also appeared in London as Mosca in the production of *Volpone* at Wilton's Music Hall. Andy has also just auditioned for the new West End musical *The Lord of the Rings*. When 'resting' he works as a temp in the accounts department of a literary agency.

'Although I worked straight after finishing my degree I didn't get to play an adult until I was 26 years old. I'm quite small and they like small people for jobs on children's TV because you seem non-threatening. I did *Sooty* for ITV and that proved to be a great job because I got loads of repeat fees for it. I've also done quite a lot of live work at places like the Nuffield

Theatre in Southampton and at BAC in London and I toured the whole of Europe in a production of *Hair!*. But the business is constantly changing and one of the biggest changes recently has been the amount of corporate work that is coming through. In the last ten years, big companies have started using actors for their major events more and more. These gigs can be very lucrative. I've been lucky enough in the past to play football with David Beckham on a

McDonald's corporate job and been paid for the privilege. I've got another one with Siemens coming up at the Carlton Studios in Nottingham where I have to play a gangster and "kidnap" the managing director. Adverts can also earn you a lot of money. I did one for a Dutch telephone company and was paid almost £2,000 for a day's work.

'Nowadays you don't absolutely need an Equity card to work because the union rules are much easier now, but I would still say to any budding actors get your Equity card because it makes you look so much more professional. The same is also true of agents. I personally do not believe you can survive without an agent. It is important to find an agent you really get on with – you wouldn't believe how many actors are scared of their agents! Spotlight offers brilliant advice on which agents to go with. Another thing you really have to do is get yourself into Spotlight – it is absolutely essential. You need to get good photos done for that, which can be expensive but they are what you are judged on so you won't get in the door without them. A showreel is also important but again, it can be very expensive but you have to speculate to accumulate in acting because you are your product and if you are marketed well then you are going to get more work.

'A lot about acting is pure blag; many actors say that they've got away with it for 20 years. You need to have a lot of self-confidence and you need to have a thick skin. Some of us are more pragmatic about it, because you can't let it get to you. Nowadays it is much more about what you look like than what you can do, which is a terrible indictment on the way the industry has gone, but it is the truth. To be successful in this.

business you have to want it more than anything else so go out there and hustle, network, write letters, keep your ear to the ground and find out who is doing which shows because people move about. Read *The Stage* and keep in contact with the actors and casting directors you work with because networking is so important.

'One of the biggest downsides to the business is being out of work. It's easy to be an actor when you are working but the true crux to being an actor is when you are resting. There's a lot of disrespect to actors, we are known as very fickle, flighty and shallow because people don't see the amount of work we have to put in just to get a job. My advice is keep your hand in by doing a course or a rehearsed reading and go and see lots of shows. You also have to have other strings to your bow. The actors I know who are the most depressed and the most unfulfilled are the ones who sit at home waiting for that call to come through. This is a difficult life and it can make you neurotic because you never know where the next pay cheque is coming from. This aspect of the life means some people run out of steam and drop out.

'It is really important to know what your strengths are. If you are good at accents and voices then radio may be a good place for you to work. If you look good, have professional management and are talented then you have the formula to succeed. I know I'm not going to get fabulously wealthy through this, recently I did panto and all the actors got paid just £300 a week, but I have had some fantastic times.'

FASCINATING FACT

The first British film to win the Oscar for Best Film was *Hamlet* way back in 1948. The great British actor Sir Laurence Olivier not only starred in the film, he also directed and produced it.

Source: *Oscar: A Pictorial History*, published by Associated Press

CHAPTER 4

Courses for Horses

Before you ever get to earn any money as an actor, first you've got to train to be one. As stated before, not every actor working in this country has been to drama school but the great majority have.

WHAT'S ON OFFER?

Creative and Cultural Skills is the sector skills council that covers the arts and entertainment industries, and Skillset, the industry organisation for training in film, TV, video and radio (see Resources) both offer comprehensive information on the wide range of NVQs (National Vocational Qualifications or SVQs in Scotland) you can now take in all the performing arts (from actor, to singer, and right up to director). Edexcel approves a number of First, National, and Higher National Diplomas and Certificates (HND/HNC) in everything from acting to make-up. These qualifications are the first step in preparing you for higher education.

You can also do degree courses in drama at universities and colleges, but many of these tend to concentrate on the academic side of the subject rather than training you in the practical aspects of stagecraft. If you graduate from one of these courses and really want to enter the profession you can do a postgraduate course at a drama school. But if you are certain you want to act or work backstage, then a vocational course specifically designed to train you as a performer or stage manager/technician is what you should be aiming for. On these you will spend many hours a day doing practical work under the supervision of experts. So the first thing you should think about when considering which college or university you wish to attend is, am I actually going to use my training to be a performer, or do I just want to study performing arts because I'm interested and will then use the skills I learn to do something else in the future?

Although you can enter training later in life (many drama schools will accept applications from people between 25 and 30 years old), by so doing you will immediately rule yourself out of some acting parts because by the time you complete your course you are going to be too old to play a person in their late teens or early twenties! You'll also be a newly qualified actor in competition with experienced actors who are the same age as you but who have already worked in the profession for years. At most drama schools the minimum age for entry to a three year course is 18, while entry age for one or two year courses is a minimum of 21.

'I'd recommend anyone to take a year off before starting on an acting course, just to get some life experience because the competition, pressure and depth of work at drama school is such you need to be older to survive. I did a secretarial course before going to RADA and it has proved invaluable.'

Kate Gielgud, actress/voice coach

Although training at a drama school can be very expensive (in some cases over £7,000 a year: at the Royal Academy of Dramatic Art (RADA) the fees for the three year BA Acting degree are currently a whopping £12,370 per year), places on these courses are always oversubscribed.

'At some (drama schools) the ratio of applicants to places is 50 to one.'

A Practical Guide To Vocational Training in Dance And Drama, published by **NCDT** and **CDET**

Although there are no formal entry requirements to many drama courses if you can show you have a keen interest in the performing arts it will do your cause no harm whatsoever. Some courses will require the equivalent of five GCSEs/S-grades and a few require two A-levels/three Scottish Highers or the equivalent. Other good qualifications to have are a BTEC National Diploma in Performing Arts, a vocational A-level in Performing Arts and Entertainment Industries, or an SQA National Certificate in Dramatic Arts or Theatre Arts. These are the requirements at Mountview Theatre Academy but it also welcomes applications from people without standard entry qualifications.

GIVING YOURSELF THE ADVANTAGE

There are already lots of things you can do while still at school to give yourself an advantage over other applicants to drama school:

- Act as much as possible. In your school play, in community theatre or youth groups, or with your local amateur dramatic society – no matter how small the part, all experience is good experience.

- Show just how interested and keen on drama you are by attending as many live performances as possible. Write your own notes on each show, paying particular attention to what you thought of the acting performances.

- Read plays, in fact, read a large variety of plays – everything from Shakespeare to Strindberg and Oscar Wilde to Tom Stoppard. Learn certain speeches by heart and discover what you feel most comfortable with – serious drama, tragedy or light comedy.

- If it is part of your school's curriculum take a GCSE in Drama or in Expressive Arts, or if you live in Scotland take a Higher or Advanced Higher in Drama.

- Join an amateur dramatic society in your area or, if you can afford to, take private drama lessons. Many young people between the ages of 13 and 21 join the National Youth Theatre (NYT). It offers courses at 13 centres around the country in acting, costume-making, lighting and sound, prop-making, and stage management and gives its members a real taste of what it is like to work in theatre as well as teaching them practical skills. NYT has an audition hotline: 0845 903 9063 (for more information see Resources).

- For a list of other amateur drama clubs and regional youth theatres contact The National Association of Youth Theatres at nayt@btconnect.com (for more information see Resources). The National Council for Drama Training also has an information sheet on youth theatre (see Resources).

- Contact your local theatre and see if it is possible to do some work experience with them. Even acting as an usher will give you a feel for the theatre experience.

- Start reading the drama reviews in your local press as well as in national newspapers. Buy *The Stage* newspaper occasionally to get a feel for the profession (see Resources).

- If you are interested in the technical aspects of theatre then start designing and making your own models, props, costumes, masks, etc., to show you have ability as well as an interest.

Most drama schools are looking for raw talent and enthusiasm, so entry is usually via one or more auditions. Some schools ask for a monologue from a play by Shakespeare or another Jacobean playwright plus a piece in clear contrast to the first.

Others will ask for an improvisation. There may well be an audition fee of £30 or £40. You will also need to go for interview so the more knowledgeable and enthusiastic about acting you are, the better.

ON COURSE 1
Typically, a three year BA Acting or Performance course will cover the following areas:

Voice, movement and physical skills
You will develop your range, projection, strength and flexibility. You may well study Alexander Technique and, if part of the course, study music theory and develop your singing and dancing.

Acting skills
You may learn Stanislavsky-based acting exercises, do improvisations and in-house presentations including classical and modern texts. By year three you will appear in public productions with invited agents and casting directors in the audience.

Add-on skills
Add-ons such as **stage combat** (both armed and unarmed) and **tumbling** may be included in your course.

Technical skills
All acting and performance degree students will be introduced to **technical crafts** as well as **radio, microphone and TV technique**. Some courses also provide **front of house** training.

Masterclass workshops
Throughout the course students will attend specialist workshops with professionals from the industry.

Audition technique
Finally, in order to get those all-important jobs, students will be trained to select suitable audition pieces and to present themselves appropriately to prospective employers.

Sources: Mountview Academy of Theatre Arts and RADA

ON COURSE 2
Typically, a two year BA or Graduate Diploma in Theatre Technical Arts will include:

Stage management
This will involve elements of **score reading, text analysis, theatre history, production and company management,** as well as **first aid** and **health and safety** at work.

Design skills
Areas covered include **set design, prop-making, wardrobe, printing** and **scenic painting.** The skills learned here will be as applicable to exhibitions, trade shows and conferences as to TV, video, film or live theatre.

Construction skills
Construction is becoming increasingly technical and so you must learn **computer-aided design** alongside the more traditional skills of **technical drawing, metalwork** and **wood turning.**

Lighting and sound
You will learn basic **electrics** along with the more technical **board operation, lighting design** and **sound design.**

By year two you will be working full time on productions for presentation to the public.

Sources: Mountview Academy of Theatre Arts and RADA

If you decide you would like a career teaching drama in the state system, you will first have to graduate and then take a course leading to a Postgraduate Certificate in Education (PGCE) in order to qualify as a teacher. You can get more information on becoming a drama teacher from the Society of Teachers of Speech and Drama (see Resources).

WHICH WAY NOW?

By now you should be clearer on what kind of course you want to apply for. If you do decide to go the vocational route, then the National Council for Drama Training (NCDT) accredits the following courses at 21 different colleges.

SCHOOL	COURSE/S	TYPE OF FUNDING
Academy of Live & Recorded Arts (ALRA)	1 Year Acting 3 Year Acting	DaDA* DaDA
Arts Educational (ArtsEd)	1 Year Acting 3 Year Acting	DaDA DaDA
Birmingham School of Acting	1 Year Acting 3 Year Acting	State-Funded HE State-Funded HE
Bristol Old Vic Theatre School	2/3 Year Acting 2/3 Year Stage Management	State-Funded HE State-Funded HE
Central School of Speech & Drama	3 Year Acting 3 Year Stage Management	State-Funded HE State-Funded HE
Drama Centre	3 Year Acting	State-Funded HE
Drama Studio	1 Year Acting	Full Fees/Independent
East 15 Acting School	1 Year Acting 1 Year Acting 3 Year Acting	Full Fees/Independent State-Funded HE State-Funded HE
Guildford School of Acting (GSA)	1 Year Acting/Musical Theatre 1 Year Stage Management 2 Year Stage Management 3 Year Acting 3 Year Musical Theatre	Full Fees/Independent Full Fees/Independent DaDA DaDA State-Funded HE
Guildhall School of Music & Drama	3 Year Acting 3 Year Stage Management	State-Funded HE State-Funded HE

SCHOOL	COURSE/S	TYPE OF FUNDING
Italia Conti Academy of Theatre Arts	3 Year Acting	State-Funded HE
London Academy of Music & Dramatic Art (LAMDA)	1 Year Acting 2 Year Stage Management 3 Year Acting	State-Funded HE State-Funded HE State-Funded HE
Manchester Metropolitan University School of Theatre	3 Year Acting	State-Funded HE
Mountview Academy of Dramatic Arts	1 Year Acting 1 Year Musical Theatre 2 Year Stage Management 3 Year Acting 3 Year Acting/Musical Theatre	DaDA DaDA DaDA DaDA DaDA
Oxford School of Drama	1 Year Acting 3 Year Acting	DaDA DaDA
Queen Margaret University College	3/4 Year Acting 3/4 Year Stage Management	State-Funded HE State-Funded HE
Rose Bruford College	3 Year Acting 3 Year Stage Management 3 Year Costume 3 Year Scenic Arts 3 Year Lighting	State-Funded HE State-Funded HE State-Funded HE State-Funded HE State-Funded HE
Royal Academy of Dramatic Art (RADA)	2 Year Stage Management 3 Year Acting	State-Funded HE State-Funded HE
Royal Scottish Academy of Music & Drama (RSAMD)	3 Year Acting 3 Year Stage Management	State-Funded HE State-Funded HE
Royal Welsh College of Music & Drama	1 Year Acting 1 Year Stage Management 3 Year Acting 3 Year Stage Management	State-Funded HE State-Funded HE State-Funded HE State-Funded HE

SCHOOL	COURSE/S	TYPE OF FUNDING
Webber Douglas Academy of Dramatic Art	1 Year Acting 3 Year Acting	DaDA State-Funded HE

*DaDA stands for Dance and Drama Awards

Source: National Council for Drama Training (NCDT).
For contact information on the above colleges you can contact NCDT direct – see Resources

FUNDING YOUR STUDIES

You will already have read about how expensive drama school training can be. This is because the courses tend to be very intensive and require input from a large number of professional teachers covering the different disciplines. However, don't panic yet and think you won't be able to afford it.

STATE-FUNDED HE COURSES

At present, students entering Higher Education pay up to £3,000 per year in tuition fees (rising to £3,070 in 2007/8). However, students from lower income backgrounds can apply for help with this fee and can also apply for student loans to cover living costs (for example, if you live at home you can apply for a living expenses loan of £3,415 rising to £6,315 if you leave home and live in London while attending your course). For more information on higher education funding, the Department for Education and Skills (DfES) publishes a guide, *Financial Support For Higher Education Students*, which is available online at www.student supportdirect.co.uk. (For more information on DfES see Resources.)

DANCE AND DRAMA AWARDS (DaDA)

DaDAs were first introduced in 1999 and they help students wishing to take approved vocational courses at independent drama schools with their fees and maintenance. But you should be aware the awards only go to the most talented students and up to 40 per cent of students on these courses have to fund their own places. The DfES has a DaDA information booklet. Contact the DfES publication line on 0845 600 9506 or at www.dfes.gov.uk/dancedrama.

Each drama school is itself responsible for allocating these awards. Your financial circumstances as well as your ability may be taken into consideration, but only as a secondary factor. DaDA students may apply for help with their student fee contribution, but they cannot apply for student loans. However, they can apply for hardship grants to help with their maintenance costs.

In England, Scotland and Wales, Manchester Education Authority processes applications for DaDA fees and maintenance. Contact the telephone enquiry service on 0161 234 7021 or write to:
The Chief Education Officer
Student Support Section
PO Box 191
Manchester M3 3ST
Email: Fund4study@notes.manchester.gov.uk

If you live in Northern Ireland you should contact:
The Department for Employment and Learning
39–49 Adelaide House
Adelaide Street
Belfast BT2 8FD
Tel: 028 9025 7777

Some courses do not attract state sector funding and for these you will be responsible for the full cost of the fees plus your own maintenance costs as you are not eligible for a loan or a grant.

FULL FEES OR INDEPENDENT COURSES

Most of the courses where you will have to find the full fees yourself are postgraduate courses or those aimed at mature students. If you are on a DaDA-funded course but fail to win a DaDA you will also have to fund the course yourself and pay your maintenance costs. Over a three year course this can add up to as much as £50,000, but do not despair, there are still alternative forms of funding out there.

Some students may be able to get a Career Development Loan (CDL) from a high street bank, where the DfES pays the interest on the loan for the length of your course. You then start paying the repayment instalments up to five months after graduation. You can get a CDL pack by contacting the DfES on 0800 585 505 or from www.lifelonglearning.co.uk.

SCHOLARSHIPS AND BURSARIES

Every student wanting to study the performing arts at a drama, music or dance school should contact their preferred schools *as early as possible*. That's because many of them have specially endowed awards schemes such as scholarships and bursaries to help students with their course fees, but you have to hurry because they are over-subscribed and only the most talented students get them. For example, RADA offers both scholarships and bursaries (acting course only) to support students in genuine financial need. At Mountview they have a number of different scholarships including the Dame Judi Dench Scholarship, the Sir John Mills Scholarship, and the Somerset Scholarship. In order to find out more about what scholarships are available you should contact drama colleges direct.

If all else fails and you are still short of funding you can apply to charitable trusts and foundations for help. This can be a long and time-consuming exercise but if you want it enough it can be found. Check your local reference library for a copy of the *Directory of Grant-Making Trusts*, published by the Charities Aid Foundation. You should also look out for *University Scholarships, Awards and Bursaries* by Brian Heap, published by Trotman. Alternatively, check out www.fundfinder.org.uk/index.php or www.scholarship-search.org.uk.

AMBER EDLIN, 32, DANCER-TURNED-ACTRESS
Amber started dance classes at the age of four at the Hillingdon Theatre Dance School and reached a high level of proficiency. She also joined a youth drama group at The Beck Theatre in Hayes and although she loved dancing she found acting more enjoyable because it combined studying text and performing. When she realised that she did not have the physicality to be a ballerina she applied to attend Guildford School of Acting on their three year acting course. Since graduating she has toured in *The Misanthrope*, appeared on the West End stage and on TV in such series as *London's Burning* and *EastEnders*.

'I didn't get a good agent immediately after I graduated and so I spent a lot of time doing fringe performances and writing off for lots of jobs. During this time I learned which venues agents will go to, and which they won't, to spot new talent. Getting a good agent in this business is very difficult unless you have some sort of personal contact who will recommend you. Once I got a good agent I felt things start to shift and went to castings more frequently.

'What I love most about acting is I am doing something I love and getting paid for it. Some days I come out of castings, especially those for commercials, and think "hang on a minute, most people are typing or serving customers and I have just been pretending to see thousands of zombies, or eat a bowl of pasta, or react to an imaginary dog". It's madness! The worst thing is the resting aspect, which can be soul destroying. In between gigs you have to get another job and I have done everything from waitressing, to teaching dance and working as a temp. It can get very frustrating because it is not what you want to do and more often than not it is not very stimulating.

'Professionally, I wish producers were a bit bolder with new names. You see the same people on TV all the time and I wish they would take more chances. I do understand that names draw audiences but come on, take a risk! In my ideal world I would play a regular character in a fantastically written sitcom or drama series (that would be lovely for the security). However, in reality, I may have to take matters into my own hands and start writing my own scripts.

'I would encourage young people to learn the skills if they really enjoy acting but they need to go into it with their eyes open to the difficulties because there seem to be more and more of us and less and less work! However, if they really have set their heart on it I would say "be confident, and GO FOR IT!"'

Finally, in this section on drama, just to prove not every dramatic person is necessarily an actor, here's someone making a living in performing arts but doing something very different indeed.

STUART SCOTT, 29, PART-TIME PROFESSIONAL MAGICIAN
After graduating from university Stuart decided not to follow the conventional graduate route. As he had always been interested in magic and magic tricks, he went to work with a German youth circus, after which he performed in two stores in London before working in Africa. Stuart still performs magic to earn extra money but on an informal basis.

'Being a professional magician was never something I wanted to do as a career but I had always been interested in magic, both as a performance art and as a mental discipline (inventing illusions involves great skill in lateral thinking). While I was at school I joined a circus club and learned a variety of related performance skills including juggling, unicycling and stilt walking. I learned magic tricks from books and through lots of practice. I also invented effects that I then performed and really the best learning came from the performing. My training was informal and a lot of fun, but training is no substitute to actually performing and learning from experience.

'Getting gigs as a magician can be difficult, especially in off-seasons. Also, getting to a good standard can take a long time and requires dedication and a lot of patience. I'd advise anyone who is seriously considering it as a career to perform as often as you can to as many different types of audience as you can. Develop your skills rather than rely on props and don't try to copy other people; develop your own style. In fact, I'd say rather than buy props, buy books on magic and devise at least one unique act and then practise it until you can do it perfectly. I'd also urge them to join a magic club to meet other magicians – you should ask their advice, but not always take it! It's also good to broaden your horizons in the performing arts. I have written, produced, acted, directed and been a theatre manager.

'Magic has gone through major changes in the UK in the last five years. In the nineties there was next to no magic on TV in the UK other than Paul Daniels. Now there has been a revival in magic brought about in part by David Blaine's first TV special and also by renewed interest in magic itself through the *Harry Potter* books and films. TV raises audiences' expectations of the performer and magicians are going to have to rise to that. There's a lot of imitation but that's because of a lack of imagination on the part of some performers. It is hard to keep up with the best magicians shown on TV but magic has the advantage of being even more impressive performed live!

'One of the best things about doing what I do is meeting people and giving them an experience they may remember for the rest of their lives. Magic is a very powerful art. A trick you've performed a thousand times in the past may be commonplace to you, but it may have a profound effect on your audience. I will always be a magician. It's more a way of seeing the world than just something you do.'

CHAPTER 5

Let's Face the Music

MUSIC UNCOVERED

It's a harmless daydream many of us indulge in from time to time: winning a TV reality show such as *X Factor* or *How Do You Solve a Problem Like Maria?* and going on to have an enormously successful (and highly lucrative) career in the music business. Unfortunately, for the vast majority of us it will always remain a dream, but if your interest in music goes beyond that of just being a fan there are plenty of jobs you can do within this sphere that may not make you rich and famous, but will definitely give you a fulfilling and rewarding career.

FASCINATING FACT

After a nationwide search, four British schoolgirls – Melanie Nakhla, Laura Wright, Charlotte Ritchie and Daisy Chute – were chosen to become All Angels, the first all-girl classical crossover group. They were signed to Universal Records last year in a £1 million record deal and released their first, self-titled album.

WHAT ARE THE JOBS?

Obviously, the people who are most visible in the music industry are the performers we see on our TV screens, in videos and at concerts. They are opera-singers like Pavarotti, rock bands such as The Darkness, easy-listening artists such as Nora Jones, or they play in orchestras such as the London Symphony Orchestra. Less visible performers include the session musicians who play the music on ads and jingles, band members in musical theatre shows such as *The Sound of Music* or *Mamma Mia!* and even high-profile DJs such as Moby or Fat Boy Slim. Only people with great talent and skill can make it as professional performers, be it as pianists, violinists or singers. According to the Office of National Statistics, 28,309 people listed their occupation as musician in 2006. If you have made up your mind to be a performer you should already be playing an instrument or having singing lessons and taking graded examinations. In fact, in order to train as a classical musician you will need Grade 8 on your main instrument and Grade 6 on a second instrument. In the world of popular music no such criteria exist and some people do make it without formal training, but these are the exception rather than the rule.

If you don't have the talent or inclination to be a performer there are still many things you can do in the music world. The music business is huge in terms of both scale and monetary value – in fact, figures from the British Phonographic Industry (BPI) for 2004 show UK record companies made £1,218.4 million in sales revenue from album sales alone (that's 237 million albums), and that's before taking into account the ticket sales for live concerts, or revenues from the sale of sheet music or instruments, and from merchandise such as T-shirts. Worldwide sales of music in the first half of 2006 topped a staggering £4.5 billion. So, you could work in a music shop selling guitars, or you could even make guitars. You could write songs or be a music journalist, work for a music publisher's office or even become a manager like Simon Cowell with your own roster of artists. Listed in the chart opposite are just some of the many jobs in the music industry that you can train to do.

JOBS IN THE MUSIC INDUSTRY

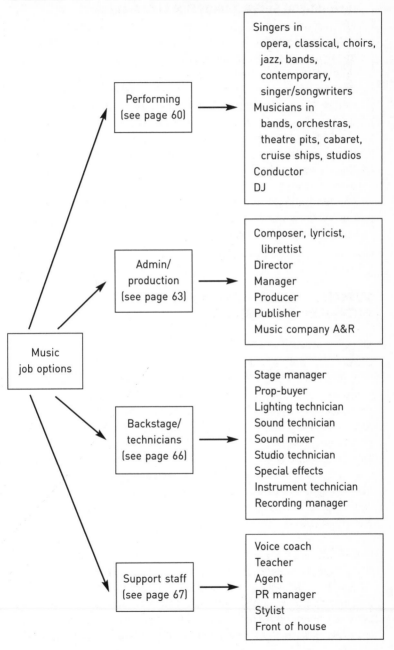

Music job options

Performing
(see page 60)

Singers in
opera, classical, choirs,
jazz, bands,
contemporary,
singer/songwriters
Musicians in
bands, orchestras,
theatre pits, cabaret,
cruise ships, studios
Conductor
DJ

Admin/production
(see page 63)

Composer, lyricist,
librettist
Director
Manager
Producer
Publisher
Music company A&R

Backstage/technicians
(see page 66)

Stage manager
Prop-buyer
Lighting technician
Sound technician
Sound mixer
Studio technician
Special effects
Instrument technician
Recording manager

Support staff
(see page 67)

Voice coach
Teacher
Agent
PR manager
Stylist
Front of house

HOW DO YOU SOLVE A PROBLEM LIKE MARIA?

When Andrew Lloyd Webber first mooted the idea of staging a West End production of film favourite *The Sound of Music*, he thought Hollywood actress Scarlett Johansson would take on the role of novice nun Maria. When this failed to happen he decided on the high-risk strategy of staging a reality TV contest to pick his leading lady. The show, *How Do You Solve a Problem Like Maria?* became a TV hit for the BBC as the original 6,000 hopefuls were whittled down to ten would-be Marias. The eventual winner, 23-year-old Connie Fisher, became a star overnight and won a standing ovation from the audience when the musical opened at the London Palladium last year. The interest in the musical that the TV show generated meant it took £12.5 million in advance box office sales.

WHEN YOU KNOW THE NOTES TO SING

Music is everywhere these days – if it's not pouring out of your CD player, radio or TV set, then it's being piped through shopping malls and lifts, or you are downloading it onto your computer or mobile telephone. Someone, somewhere, has to compose that music, play it and record it. The public usually only sees the glamorous face of the music business in the form of the performers up there on stage, be they playing a violin concerto or a piece of rock music, but many of the jobs within the industry are unglamorous and extremely hard work. As in the acting world there are some aspects of the music industry you need to have a long think about before deciding if this is the world for you.

INSECURITY

Of the approximately 2,150 people who graduated from music studies in 2002, only 54 per cent went straight into employment, and of these only 34 per cent went into full-time paid work in the UK (data supplied by the Higher Education Statistics Agency (HESA)). This means there are a lot of music graduates out there

who did not find work. The music world is notoriously fluid and
fickle, so a particular job in music will not necessarily be 'for life'.
You must be prepared to move around from job to job and to
sustain periods of unemployment. If you are a performer you may
have to teach or do session work in order to supplement your
earnings. If you work in other areas of the industry, such as a
record company, you may well find yourself frequently moving
around departments and from concentrating on one artist to
another. This certainly makes life challenging, but not everybody
enjoys such insecurity and instability in their working lives. If you
would like a more structured career you should seriously think
about jobs that may be connected to the industry but are less
closely linked to the performing side.

LOW INCOME

We will explore the money you can make in music in more detail
in Chapter 6, where you will find a box listing some of the huge
sums of money musicians can earn, but you should be aware that
these are the people at the top of their profession. For every
Yehudi Menuhin, Charlotte Church or The Darkness there are
countless struggling violinists, opera-singers or rock groups
earning fairly low wages. For instance, if you are a musician in an
orchestra, the annual rate of pay starts at around £13,500. If you
work as a freelancer you may be contracted to do a very lucrative
tour for six months of the year and then not work again for a
further three months. Equity minimum wages for musicians are
just £319 a week for opera-singers, while a singer performing
eight times a week in a West End show can expect to get paid
£366.82. A session singer performing for the BBC or ITV earns
£159 for a three hour session, while session singers for radio
commercials earn £125 for a one hour session. Although the
potential for earning a good wage should be important to you, the
primary reason you should be in this business is because you love
it. There is too much competition for jobs in this industry for you
to make a success of it if you don't feel passionately about what
you do.

BOREDOM

You may think boredom is a strange thing to bring up when
discussing the exciting world of music, but jobbing musicians
will tell you boredom can seriously affect the enjoyment they get

from what they do. For example, say you are employed playing guitar in a band that is hired out for parties, weddings, bar mitzvahs and corporate dos. You will have a repertoire of songs you perform and not only will you rehearse these songs intensely but also you will end up playing the same songs night after night. There are only so many times you can play 'Lady In Red' before it ceases to thrill you. This is particularly true when the music you are playing is not to your own personal taste. Playing the same pieces many times over can sap your enthusiasm and so you really have to be dedicated for it not to affect your performances adversely.

'If you have a family and a pension and a mortgage then the boredom of playing the same thing week in, week out on a long-running show in the West End is only offset by the knowledge you are financially secure.'

Carlton Edwards, Musical Director

ANTISOCIAL HOURS

No one working in the performing arts area can expect to work a standard 9am to 5pm day – it just isn't like that. Performers tend to work while the public enjoys its leisure hours; this means in the evenings and at weekends. Even if you are a session musician working in a studio, you will often carry on playing until you get it right, which could be well into the night, and the same goes for bands recording their albums. You could be on tour so, on top of the hours you put in performing, you will also have to take into account the hours spent on the road getting from venue to venue. Non-performers such as A&R (artist and repertoire) scouts, roadies, tour managers and press officers have to work around the performers so they too will be putting in long and often antisocial hours. If you want to be at home in time to put your feet up and watch your favourite TV soap each night, then this is definitely the wrong industry for you.

> **FASCINATING FACT**
>
> **In the first half of 2006 digital music sales soared by 106 per cent to £945 million, while sales of CDs dropped.**
> **Source: Recording industry group IFPI**

MAKING MUSIC

If none of the above puts you off making a career for yourself in the music business, then you already have one of the personal attributes that will help you be a success – determination – and there are other strengths, both personal and physical, that will help you get on. It goes without saying that natural ability and talent are two key attributes for musical performers.

SOCIABILITY

Even if you are a solo artist, such as a singer/songwriter, you are going to need other people around you to help you make the music you want to. This is especially true if you are in an orchestra, a jazz band, a choir or any other form of group. You need to have good people skills, be able to interact and get on easily with other people. Life on the road, when you are touring, can get really intense so if you can keep a smile on your face and not fall out with people you will be an asset rather than a pain.

'Because it is a small, close world in the musical theatre end of the business, musicians, singers, dancers, choreographers and directors tend to go from show to show so you can't afford to make enemies. Because I'm personable, can get on with people and am well-liked, people want to keep on hiring me.'

Carlton Edwards, Musical Director

CREATIVITY

In the music world you really do have to 'think outside of the box'. If you are a songwriter or composer you will be using your creativity each and every day. A music manager will have to spot trends and think of imaginative ways to market his or her acts, and music teachers must come up with novel methods to keep their pupils interested and motivated.

STAMINA

Don't be fooled into thinking the music industry is all about having a lark; this is a serious business and in order to make it you are going to have to work long and hard. You have to put in the hours of practice, you may have to play every night, and the work is often exhausting (just imagine the concentration needed to play live Philip Glass's opera piece 'Einstein On The Beach', which lasts five hours). You need to be physically fit and mentally alert, so you are going to have to look after yourself.

COMPUTER SKILLS

Many musicians now write and record music using software packages such as CUBASE so you need to be computer literate. This is especially true if you want to be a keyboard player, a sequencer, remixer or DJ where you will be sampling sounds electronically. Record companies have websites for their artists and for such things as back catalogue, while many ticket agencies such as Ticketmaster now accept bookings for concerts via the internet, so make sure your computer skills are up to scratch.

ORGANISATIONAL SKILLS

Putting on any kind of musical performance can be a logistical nightmare, so the last thing anyone needs is for you to be disorganised. You need to be in certain places at certain times, you need to have practised until you are perfect, and you need to know what the people around you are also doing, so get yourself sorted! There is too much money involved in the business for things to go wrong; if you can help things run smoothly by having good organisational skills then people will be more inclined to employ you time and time again.

COMMON SENSE

Being level-headed and having your feet placed firmly on the ground are great strengths to possess whatever career in music you plan to have. This is a fast-moving, often stressful world where people work under pressure. If you can keep your wits about you, stay calm and think things through logically, then people will know they can rely on you in a crisis. Creative people sometimes have a reputation for flakiness; make sure you have a reputation for using your common sense and you'll go far.

TEAM WORK

You really have to be a team-player to get ahead in music. Basically, this is because so many roles within the music industry depend on working with other people. Music groups work as a team, roadies work as a team, and your management group *is* your team. You will need good communication skills and the ability to take orders as well as to give them. The higher up the ladder of responsibility you get the more you have to learn to delegate and if you have a good working relationship with those around you they will be more inclined to share the burden of responsibility with you.

FASCINATING FACT

2006 saw a revival of fortunes for British music acts. According to the British Phonographic Industry, British artists created 62 per cent of the top-selling albums with seven British acts in the top ten albums (Snow Patrol was at number one with the reformed Take That at number two). Significantly, debut albums by British bands were also hitting the big time with the Arctic Monkeys' *Whatever People Say I Am, That's What I'm Not* **becoming the fastest-selling debut of all time and winning them the Mercury Music Prize.**

WILL YOU MAKE THE GRADE?

Just as there are strengths that will help you achieve your ambitions in music, so too are there weaknesses that could hold you back. Once again, this section is primarily aimed at performers and those in the positions closest to them. As you move away from this core group, these weaknesses become less relevant so if you do suffer from any of the following, you could still work in the music industry but in non-performance-related roles.

TONE DEAFNESS

We would all like to believe we have perfect pitch but the unfortunate fact is the majority of us don't. If you can't hold a tune to save your life, let alone find middle C, you probably already know making music is not for you. This is as true for people who play musical instruments as it is for singers because they very often 'play by ear' rather than read music. Although there is, apparently, a current trend for R&B and hip hop acts to be out of tune (e.g. Lumidee and Outkast's Andre 3000) there is no guarantee this fad will last any longer than other musical fads.

PERFORMANCE STRESS

If the thought of going out on stage and performing in front of thousands of people brings you out in a cold sweat there's little chance of you ever appearing at the Glastonbury Festival or the Brit Awards. Panic attacks and nerves will seriously affect your ability to perform – the vocal chords become constricted and you'll suddenly find you are playing with two left hands. Some people find that although they simply can't perform in front of a live audience, they are fine in a recording studio or orchestra pit where the audience can't see them. Others find performance stress becomes less of a problem or disappears completely the more they perform live. If you are in a school band take the opportunity to appear in as many shows or competitions as possible; this will give you an indication of whether nerves are going to get the better of you or not.

PRONENESS TO INJURY

Musicians really need to look after themselves. The human voice must be nurtured and nursed as serious throat infections or conditions such as nodules on the vocal chords can ruin promising singing careers (Julie Andrews of *Mary Poppins* and *The Sound of Music* has been told she must never sing again because of nodules). Most musicians play their instruments with their hands so they have to be careful to watch out for such conditions as RSI (repetitive strain injury) and arthritis and try their hardest not to damage them. Carlton Edwards had to give up the idea of becoming a concert pianist after two injuries to his hands (falling through a cold frame and a plate glass window), although he still works in the industry (see the case study opposite).

LACK OF SELF-ESTEEM

This is an industry that can really knock your self-confidence for six. What if nobody likes the songs you sing or the music you make? If you go up to audition for a part in the latest musical in the West End with ten other performers and don't even get into the chorus line you can start to doubt your own ability. DON'T! Once you start to doubt yourself you won't have the confidence to convince others of your talents and skills. Self-belief is all in this game: remember, the product you are marketing is you, so go out there with the hard sell.

FASCINATING FACT

Rock singer Abigail Holdsworth has become the first musician to finance her debut single by dividing its cover into squares and selling each subsequent advertising space for £150. She has so far made £20,000.

CARLTON EDWARDS, MUSICAL DIRECTOR/COMPOSER

Carlton started playing the piano at 4 years old. He was set to do a Music and Drama degree at Hull University and took a year out to work in London before starting the course. Here he found employment playing the piano in hotel foyers and also in private clubs and so he never took up his university place. Since then he has worked in the music industry constantly, first writing for a jingle company, then performing his own songs and playing piano for rehearsals, and more recently as assistant musical director on West End shows such as *Oliver!*, *Mamma Mia!*, *Chitty Chitty Bang Bang* and *The Full Monty*. In 2005/6 he became the musical director for the international touring production of *Mamma Mia!* visiting much of Europe and South Africa. Since then he has been musical director for a children's show entitled *The Wolves in the Walls*, and also went to Russia for a month to help record all the backing vocals for *Mamma Mia!* in Russian.

'Writing for the jingle company was brilliant because it gave me both studio and engineering experience with sequencers and drum machines. I think everyone in the business should be learning new crafts within their sphere – there is always something new you can learn. That experience taught me my backstage skills are far better than my performing on stage skills and so I went on a tour with a group of students from a theatre school where I acted as musical director (MD), playing piano and making sure the cast were all singing in tune and looking after themselves. After that, a friend who was the MD on *Oliver!* rang to ask me to play the piano in the rehearsals when they had a cast change and the new cast members had to learn all their song parts and dance steps. From there I went on a tour of Canada with *Oliver!* and that is where I started to conduct the show and when I got back to England I went on to become assistant MD on *Mamma Mia!*.

'The assistant MD usually plays the piano in the band in the pit and will normally play for six of the eight shows a week and then conduct the other two shows a week. He or she also has responsibility for rehearsals so you are always in the building and always busy. It can be enjoyable but it is pretty full on because you tend to have to pick up the pieces other people don't want to do. I like MDing – I like actors, I like people and I like working with music. For most of us who work in the West End, our days are free and once the show is up and running and you are comfortable with the performance side then you do have time for other things, but one of the downsides of the job is that the hours are all round the wrong way. Some people take to working in the evenings but some do not. You have to be a nocturnal person. There is also performance pressure, and fear of failure because if you are MDing a show for people's entertainment then you want to make it as good as possible and that is stressful. It can be terrifying doing a show in a 2,000 seat theatre but you have to get over your fear otherwise it just becomes a nightmare in your head. What you have to say to yourself is this is just a theatre and it's just a band and everyone is helping each other. The worst that could happen is that the show stops – you're not packing parachutes.

'For this job you absolutely have to have people-management skills. It's all about social skills and pastoral care because to make the show successful you have to make sure your band is happy and your cast stays healthy. That's why a good MD always puts themselves last in the equation because if you are good at your job then you are strong enough and emotionally sorted enough to take on board the things that go wrong. Being a good musician is not enough, you have to be a psychiatrist, nursemaid and all round people person as well.

'Obviously, MDing is a full-time job, but you often find musicians have other outlets for their talents. I do a lot of youth work during the days and other people I know do gigs or concerts and they teach as well. It's really good for young people to have musicians who are actually working in the business teaching them because you know what is going on.

'Whatever you end up doing, you have to take it seriously, have fun but work hard and above all, practise! This career really is a vocation because it is so linked in with your hobby and pastimes and interests. If you are a good musician working in the industry you really will have to love what you do which means choosing your jobs carefully. Getting a job on a show with a long run may be financially secure but it can become boring playing the same thing week in and week out. I've seen some very good players lose their self-esteem because they hate the music they are playing every night. However, if you are adaptable, have ability and are realistic it really can be a financially and personally rewarding job.'

JOBS IN THE MUSIC INDUSTRY

You should have a good idea by now of what it takes to be a success in the music industry and you may know exactly which job within the industry you want. If you haven't started playing an instrument already or taking singing lessons, then becoming a performer may be extremely difficult, especially in classical music. However, this industry is huge and there are plenty of other careers you can pursue in music. The chart on page 49 lists a few of the job options available, and here we look at some of them in more detail.

PERFORMING

You can basically break down musical performers into the following two groups.

MUSICIANS

Musicians need to be extremely competent players. There are five main categories of instruments: brass, keyboard, percussion, strings and wind, and some musicians play more than one instrument and also sing (Sting can play guitar and double bass). Most professional musicians need to be able to sight-read music, especially those working in orchestras. You could be a pianist, a drummer or a violin player and the range of groups, bands and orchestras you can play in is astonishing. On the classical side there are extremely large symphony orchestras, or the orchestras attached to opera or ballet companies, string quartets, chamber groups and ensembles. Only very exceptional players have the talent and the emotional strength to become soloists. Many musicians working in classical music are employed on a freelance or contract basis where the contracts can run for one tour or a number of years.

On the popular music side the range is even greater, because 'popular' covers everything from jazz, folk and country to rap, soul and pop. You can play in large swing bands, rock groups and jazz quartets. You can also play in a military band or in the pit for musical theatre. You could be a session musician who spends the whole time working in a recording studio doing everything from jingles to guest appearances on someone else's album. Again, many are freelance. As a musician you can expect to work in a variety of different locations including practice rooms, studios, jazz clubs, music halls and auditoriums, and if you are part of a show band you may well perform in marquees at weddings, parties and big events.

SINGERS

Singers also have a lot of job opportunities open to them. On the classical side there are choirs, and opera and operetta companies. You can be part of the chorus (the main body of singers), or you can be a soloist. Once again, soloists must have exceptional talent and will spend years training their voice. Popular music vocalists may or may not have had traditional vocal training and either sing as part of a band, as backing singers or as soloists. Many singers are also musicians such as Chris Martin (Coldplay), Tori Amos and Jamie Cullum who all sing and play piano. Some specialise in session work in studios, while most will mix live work at concerts with a recording career.

Other performers include DJs, who remix records by other people at live events and in clubs. Many have no traditional musical training at all, but they need to have expert computer skills and be up to date with technology that is changing rapidly. For instance, most DJs used to use vinyl records to do their mixes, but new CD mixers are now taking over. Fat Boy Slim, Moby and Judge Jules are just some of the DJs earning very large sums for their services. You might not think of a conductor as being a performer but there he or she is, up on stage waving the baton. Many conductors are actually musicians with many years' experience. They will choose the pieces an orchestra plays, rehearse with the orchestra and, on performance nights, ensure the orchestra is in time, on the beat and is conveying the right emotions through the music. They have to be able to sight-read and have a deep understanding of music theory.

Tastes in popular music are said to have a seven year cycle. Three of the biggest trends in the last few years have been: the renaissance of the rock guitar band such as The Darkness; the public's voracious appetite for musical theatre (new musicals in the West End include *Daddy Cool*, *The Sound of Music*, *Dirty Dancing*, *Spamalot* and *The Lord of the Rings*); and the total dominance of the UK charts by AOR (adult-orientated rock) or easy-listening acts such as Dido and David Gray. Next year it could be something entirely different, so if you want to be a performer it pays to be flexible and to have a broad range of musical skills.

BEHIND THE SCENES AT THE LORD OF THE RINGS
The Lord of the Rings will open in the West End at the Theatre Royal Drury Lane on Tuesday 19 June 2007. The production has book and lyrics by Shaun McKenna and Matthew Warchus and music by A. R. Rahman and Värttinä with Christopher Nightingale. The show will be directed by Matthew Warchus, with choreography by Peter Darling.

Matthew Warchus graduated from Bristol University with a First Class honours degree in Music and Drama with Special Distinction – the first ever awarded by the university. He immediately began a very busy career as a director, which has to date encompassed over 50 major stage productions (35 award-winning), including five operas and one feature film.

Indian composer A. R. Rahman is one of the most successful artistes of all time and, according to a BBC estimate, has sold more than 100 million albums of his works, comprising of music from more than 50 films. In 2001, Andrew Lloyd Webber invited Rahman to compose for the musical *Bombay Dreams*, which opened to packed houses in London's West End.

Värttinä is Finland's most successful contemporary folk music group, now celebrating their 23rd year and the release of their 11th album, *Miero*. Fronted by three female singers and supported by six acoustic musicians, Värttinä composes most of their music and lyrics based on traditional Karelian and other Finno-Ugric styles but with modern and thoroughly distinctive and original arrangements.

Peter Darling choreographed *Billy Elliot The Musical* and the Madness musical *Our House*.

THEIR BIG BREAK

Sometimes, just being in the right place at the right time can be the factor that turns a promising young performer into a real success story. Here is how four new stars got their big breaks:

- Devonshire teen Joss Stone was first noticed when she appeared on BBC TV's *Star for a Night*. Since then she has recorded her critically acclaimed debut album *The Soul Sessions* at Florida's famous TK studios, and can now count Tom Cruise as one of her biggest fans.

- Jazz-inspired pianist and vocalist Jamie Cullum became the subject of a bidding war after he sang on Michael Parkinson's Saturday night TV show in 2003. Universal eventually signed him for a £1 million deal.

- Nineteen-year-old Katie Melua is the protégée of veteran producer Mike Batt. Katie attended the Brit School for Performing Arts in Croydon where she studied a BTEC and a music A-level. Her debut album *Call Off the Search* was championed by Radio 2 and knocked Dido's *Life For Rent* off the top spot in the UK charts.

- Sixteen-year-old Erin Rocha was doing work experience at a Hampshire studio when she was asked if she could sing on a demo for a song called 'Can't do Right For Doing Wrong', a song intended for Nora Jones. Erin's version made it onto the A-playlist at BBC Radio 2 and she has subsequently been signed by EMI.

ADMINISTRATION/PRODUCTION

WRITERS AND COMPOSERS

No musical performer could do their job without the composers, lyricists and librettists who write the material they perform. In fact, in popular music many performers are actually singer/songwriters using their own material. However, some songwriters don't wish to perform themselves and write exclusively for other people. Some work in songwriting pairs where one person writes the music and the other person writes the lyrics. Famous songwriting pairs include Gilbert and Sullivan (light opera), Elton John and Bernie Taupin (pop) and Andrew Lloyd Webber and Tim Rice (musical theatre). If you are writing for the popular market you must take into account musical trends and fads, otherwise your songs will not sell. In fact, the singles market, at one time a lucrative area for songwriters, is currently in freefall and many radio stations now play album tracks rather than singles.

ANDY SPIEGEL, ACTOR/CASTING DIRECTOR
Once seen as terribly old-fashioned, folk singers made a comeback in 2006 with Kate Rusby singing the title song to BBC TV's *Jam and Jerusalem* series, while a Findlay Brown track was used on the Mastercard Christmas advert, and harpist Joanna Newsom's 'This Side of the Blue' was used on an Orange mobile advert. Meanwhile, fellow folkie Seth Lakeman was nominated for the Mercury Music Prize.

PRODUCTION
Also close to the heart of the music-making process is the producer. He or she works in the recording studio at the mixing desk and is responsible for the sound of the finished songs or musical piece. He or she will add effects, increase the bass or soften the vocals in order to get the perfect mix. A good producer works incredibly closely with the musicians and singers and needs to have great empathy with them, coaxing out the best performances and suggesting different sounds or styles that will give their material that unique edge. Many producers are also musicians themselves, although some come up through being studio engineers learning the art of production on the job. Many pop acts become so attached to their producers they use them for all their recorded work.

MANAGEMENT
Just as important – and feared by many – is the all-powerful music manager. Anyone watching Simon Cowell demolish a would-be performer on *Pop Idol* will know managers speak their

minds. They have to – it's their job. They are there to get the best deals for their acts, the most coverage in the media and to secure the best venues for them to play. They will liaise with the band or solo artist, with music companies and music publishers as well as organise tours, gigs, video shoots and TV appearances. For many the manager is God and for their troubles they will take a percentage of your earnings from records, tours and other promotional appearances.

'Managers such as Simon Fuller (Spice Girls and S Club 7) play an important role in shaping and developing their clients' careers . . . Professional managers are often the interface between the artist and record companies, music publishers, tour promoters, merchandisers and professional advisors, and they can command gross commission rates typically of 15 per cent and 20 per cent of artists' earnings.'

'Counting The Notes', published by the National Music Council

PUBLISHING COMPANIES

Talking of money, the publisher or publishing company is a really important part of a musician's team. This is because they make sure you get all the monies you are owed for your songs and music. This happens in two ways. Firstly, you earn money from your music every time it is played on the TV or on the radio, in shopping malls or in lifts. A body called the Performing Rights Society (PRS) is responsible for collecting this money. Secondly, you also earn money from every CD, DVD and record that you sell. This money is collected by the Mechanical Copyright Protection Society (MCPS). The publisher will make sure all this money comes back to you. Some artists get publishing deals before they get a recording contract and the publisher will help them get media exposure.

DIRECTORS

In musical theatre the musical director does roughly the same job as a conductor in classical music, however his or her remit tends to be broader. They will take charge in the orchestra pit and also play an instrument (normally the keyboard). They are responsible for rehearsals and sorting out any problems, so need to be at the theatre for considerable periods of time and not just for the performances.

BACKSTAGE/TECHNICIANS

Mounting any type of musical production, be it a rock concert tour, an opera at Glyndebourne, a video shoot, a TV appearance or a classical show, involves the work of a lot of people you will never see, but whose absence you would notice if they weren't doing their jobs.

In theatres, stage managers are the logisticians, ensuring everything is where it should be, sourcing props and making sure the production doesn't go over budget. The lighting technicians are responsible for both designing and rigging the lights, which can be extremely sophisticated, while the sound technicians are responsible for the microphones, the amplifiers and the mixing desk, ensuring the perfect quality of the sound. Most large bands these days also have instrument technicians who make sure the guitars, keyboards and drums are all in tune and undamaged. Meanwhile, the roadies are responsible for the safe arrival, repackage and transport of all the technical gear – including the lighting and sound equipment and any props being used. Other people that are essential to opera and musical theatre are set designers, make-up and hair departments, costume designers and wardrobe staff.

In the recording studio, the manager is responsible for getting acts into the studio and using the facilities, so they need good contacts with record companies and also with agents. They may be responsible for the bookings system and will certainly coordinate the studio staff, the producers and the bands, and make sure the studio or studios have the most up-to-date equipment that is in good working order. Engineers need a lot of technical knowledge because they have to make certain everything is running smoothly, from the microphones to the mixing desk and recording equipment. Studio time can be enormously expensive so acts need to know they are not going to arrive and discover a problem. Engineers may employ the help of assistant engineers and tape operatives (ops).

SUPPORT STAFF

At the big record companies, a number of people are responsible for the well-being of their artists. These include the label manager who will sort out what type of budget is to be spent on each group and will help groom each act for success; the A&R people who scout for new acts and hire them, then advise them on their career direction and progression; and the press officers responsible for sending out press releases, demo copies of records, arranging interviews on TV, radio and in newspapers and magazines, and accompanying their artists when they make public appearances.

Some of the more successful artists may have their own stylists who choose their clothes for them to wear on stage, in videos and at award ceremonies, and arrange to 'borrow' outfits from designers for them to wear.

Voice coaches and music teachers are a vital part of the music industry, as you should never stop learning. The majority of music teachers are classically trained. If you want to teach music at a state school you need to become a qualified teacher. If you are a graduate you can achieve this by taking a one year Postgraduate Certificate in Education (PGCE). If you want to concentrate on singing coaching or the teaching of a specific instrument, you can take a teaching or a performance diploma.

RELATED ROLES

If you really want to work in the music business but have no musical skills you could always work for a ticket office or ticket agent such as Ticketmaster. You could work on merchandising, selling the T-shirts, posters and baseball caps of famous artists to their fans. Some people become promoters, booking venues and selling tickets to concerts. Others become radio DJs, TV presenters, public relations managers and music journalists, simply because they love music, even if they can't make it as a performer.

TANIA PEACH, 34, PRODUCTION MANAGER, MOUNTVIEW THEATRE ACADEMY

Tania took Technical Theatre at Rose Bruford College but left early when she was offered a job with a company specialising in outdoor trapeze and theatre and toured extensively in Europe with them. She also worked with Oxfordshire Touring and Paynes Plough before joining Mountview in 2003. Tania is doing an MA in Arts Administration and Cultural Policies with a view to going into general and venue management.

'Here at Mountview we do approximately 16 productions a year and it's a pretty hectic schedule. I have to oversee the freelancers we bring in to work on the shows as well as the students who staff the shows. I have to coordinate the scheduling, the budgeting for the staff, and the production budget for the show. I do a lot of venue liaison and even though I don't generate the contracts I operate the contracts with the venues making sure their staff don't go into overtime. There is a lot of logistics in terms of van movements, people movements and equipment movements. Creatively I work quite closely with the directors and the designers before they even go into rehearsals. We look at the parameters and see how we can make the design work in the space available. I'm basically responsible for the practical input of the design.

'The two performance courses I deal with the most are the undergraduate acting course and the musical theatre course. We do a cross-section of shows, from Shakespeare to Brecht, to fairly large-scale musicals, which is why we tend to go to outside venues because they have better facilities for flying, etc, than we do here. One of the most important skills I bring to my job is being able to see the big picture, the overview, and another is people management. You definitely need communication skills too.

'Another important skill is being able to marry artistic ideas with practicalities and budgets. I used to think of the financial aspect of the job as a necessary evil, but now I quite enjoy it; I actually find it quite creative. A grasp of the financial side is essential because you work quite a lot with spreadsheets and Excel and you have to stay on top of it.

'Some of the worst things about the job are that you work very long, antisocial hours on fairly low budgets and so you are trying to perform miracles half of the time. There are times when the artistic side just won't marry with the practical side.

'I've always believed strongly in the creative element of the technician's role and how one collaborates and on what level. You are facilitating the work of the creatives and yet quite often your decisions as a technician inform the actual work. It is all interactive.

'The technical courses at Mountview really are like being in the industry; this is as close to the industry standard as you could possibly get, so if a student can do this they will be able to go straight out and get jobs in the industry. All the tutors are encouraged to keep abreast of what is going on as far as industry practice and contacts are concerned, because contacts are so important and we will get students work if we possibly can.'

CHRIS MARTIN, 24, 2ND YEAR TECHNICAL THEATRE DEGREE STUDENT SPECIALISING IN LIGHTING DESIGN
Chris has always been interested in drama and after doing Drama GCSE he started working front of house at a theatre. Part of the job involved frequent meetings with the backstage technicians and he liked what they did so much he too started working backstage. Through his work experience Chris received a scholarship to Mountview Theatre Academy.

'I do love performing but I want this job as a career and acting is so unpredictable so I decided to take up technical and keep acting as my hobby. As much as I love the theatre I am actually looking for work outside that field, so I'm exploring doing lighting for concerts, gigs and big clubs. In fact, I'm off to Israel as soon as I finish at Mountview to work as the head of lighting for a big sound company. They hire out equipment for hotels and events such as discos, concerts and corporate events.

'I think the best thing about what I do is the sense of achievement you get after a show. To have your lighting design viewed on stage or set and to have someone say your lights were good is a great thrill. For my job you need to be really creative and you have to have an eye for design, vision and a strong imagination. With lighting design it is all trial and error. You can draw something up but you won't know what it looks like until you've actually tried it out on set. You really have to understand what you are working with and what you are working towards.

'These days when you do a show the technical staff get the same respect for what they are doing as the actual performers because let's face it, they wouldn't be able to do the show without you. More and more, people are appreciating the backstage input into shows, especially as they get more technically complex and spectacular.

'I can't really think of any downsides to the industry, although the financial side is not that good when you first start out. A lighting technician straight from college will probably only earn between £13,000 and £16,000, however you can earn substantial sums as you get more experienced. Sometimes big egos can cause a problem but in the theatre industry there is very little leeway for mistakes and that makes people sort out their problems very quickly. Here at Mountview they drum into us that we are working as a company and they teach us how to deal with ego problems and control them.

'Ultimately, I'd like to be a lighting consultant and a touring designer. I'd like to be the person people come to and say, "what can we do about this?". I want to do big events. I'm planning to take a one year City & Guilds qualification in electronics because I know that will help with my understanding of the equipment.

'My advice to anyone thinking about doing this as a career is go and see shows because you need to understand the basics. Get involved: get a job in front of house at your local theatre; join an amateur dramatic society; or volunteer to help out backstage. All of those experiences will really help you.'

MIKE NICHOLS, 37, PROFESSIONAL BASS PLAYER

Mike first became seriously interested in music when he was 14 years old. After doing his O-levels he took A-levels in Music and History. From school he went to Leeds College of Music and took his Graduate Diploma and he subsequently took a Postgraduate Diploma in Music from Guildhall. Mike now plays electric bass as well as the traditional double bass on a freelance basis.

'College gave me the necessary skills to become a professional musician and the opportunity to get to know other people in the business. After college I started touring clubs, mostly in the north of England and Wales. I also worked with function bands and on the local jazz scene in Leeds. At this time I also did some private teaching.'

Mike then decided to move from Leeds down to London where he continued to work with function bands and played backing for cabaret artistes. He also did some work on cruise ships (a very lucrative gig, if you can get it!) and played around London's network of small jazz clubs. Although he still works with a variety of different bands he has now moved more into theatre work, both touring and in the West End, and has also done some college lecturing.

'On a day-to-day basis I could be at home writing or arranging a piece of music, or I could be working in a theatre or lecturing at college. Alternatively, I could be travelling to anywhere in the world to perform with a band. This is what I like the most about what I do – the variety of the work and the constant new challenges. However, the downside is that it's a way of life that can conflict with family and relationships. It is difficult to keep regular hours and sometimes leads to sleep deprivation!'

Ultimately, Mike would like to do more creative and studio work. He'd also like to get better gigs, paying more money, and have the luxury of being able to pick and choose the gigs he does do.

'I think the main things you need to make a success of music as a career are tenacity, confidence and respect for other people. If you want to be a musician forget it! But if you've got to be a musician it's the best job in the world.'

CHAPTER 6

Singing for Your Supper

As with all the other performing arts, a job for life in music may be hard to come by. This is why nearly every musician and singer will have skills that make it possible for them to find alternative employment when the musical pickings are slim. The only good thing about working in the evenings is that it leaves your days free to earn money by teaching or doing session work. Some people can and do make an awful lot of money from music, as illustrated in the box on the next page, but you should not bet on that happening to you.

WHAT WILL YOU EARN?

The Musicians' Union recommends basic pay rates for musicians and you may be surprised at how modest they are (the figures quoted here are a guideline only). The minimum for a musician in an armed forces band is around £13,000, while members of orchestras earn from £13,500. If you are working freelance the minimum rate is £53 for a two hour gig before midnight, while solo musicians on tour earn between £500 and £2,000 a week depending on their experience and the project they are working on. A backing singer working on an album should earn a minimum of £110 for three hours and £125 for a one hour session on a radio commercial. Obviously, rates within the West End tend to be higher. Opera-singers earn a minimum of £319 a week, however those at the Royal Opera in Covent Garden earn up to £655 a week. A musician in the pit for a West End show earns a minimum of £629.37 a week. This works out at approximately 20 hours of playing time, as well as all the other work you do on top.

Positions in the West End are fiercely competitive because there are so few seats available (*Miss Saigon* employed 27 musicians, *Oliver!* employed 25 and *Chitty Chitty Bang Bang* employed just 19). The same is true in opera as there are so few jobs available. For instance, in 2000, according to the Arts Council of England, just 556 artistic staff were employed on a permanent basis in major opera companies in the country, while 1010 artistic staff were employed on a contract or freelance basis.

WE'RE IN THE MONEY:
EARNINGS OF THE TEN WEALTHIEST BRITISH ACTS IN 2003

1. The Rolling Stones (£55.3 million)

2. Sir Paul McCartney (£40 million)

3. Sir Elton John (£34 million)

4. Robbie Williams (£30 million)

5. Coldplay (£25.3 million)

6. Sting (£25.14 million)

7. Phil Collins (£25.12 million)

8. Fleetwood Mac (£23.5 million)

9. Iron Maiden (£17.9 million)

10. Dido (£15.8 million)

Source: *Heat*; based on record sales, DVDs, touring, royalties, merchandising and other income

---

SCHOOL OF ROCK

If you have really decided that a career in music is for you then, as a performer, there are some things you should already be doing:

- If you want to be a musician you should be playing at least one instrument in the school band or orchestra (if there is one) and taking graded examinations.

- If you want to be a singer you should already be in your school choir or choral group (if there is one) and taking lessons and graded examinations.

- If possible, enter competitions such as the BBC's 'Young Musician of the Year'.

- There may well be an amateur operatic company in your area that could do with some help. Offer your services. The same is true if your local amateur dramatic society does musical productions.

- Some music colleges, like the Royal College of Music (RCM), offer opportunities and training to gifted students up to the age of 18. The RCM's Junior Department operates on Saturdays only and is an intense and very high-quality course of study, training and workshops. Only extremely talented students are accepted and there may be financial assistance for successful candidates.

- Above all you must **practise**. This is a career where dedication, energy, focus and hard work will really pay dividends.

Creative and Cultural Skills and Skillseekers can offer advice on S/NVQs and Apprenticeships within the world of music (Edexcel has a number of courses it approves including a BTEC First Diploma in Performing Arts (Music) and both a National Certificate and a National Diploma in Performing Arts (Musical Theatre); see Resources. These will all be extremely useful if you decide to take a degree in music where you will also normally need two A-levels (including Music) as entrance requirements (for classical music courses you also need Grade 8 on your first instrument and Grade 6 on your second). The Apprenticeship programme in Arts and Entertainment offered by Creative and Cultural Skills in England and Wales tend to be more on the practical side (working in a studio or backstage) where the apprentice receives training on the job while earning a wage. Normally, training is up to Key Stage 4 and is only open to people between 16 and 24 years old. If you are interested in an Apprenticeship contact your local Learning and Skills Council (LSC) in England and Wales, or Local Enterprise Council (LEC) in Scotland (see Resources).

If you are seriously considering taking a music degree do bear in mind that of the 2,150 students who graduated in music in 2002, around 750 continued in further study or training (about 35 per cent) rather than going straight into employment. Of these a third took teacher training courses, either in the shape of the Postgraduate Certificate in Education (necessary if you want to teach in a state school), or teaching or performance diplomas if they wanted to teach singing or an instrument in the private sector (Source: the Higher Education Statistics Agency). Other postgraduate courses include PhDs in Music Technology, Musical Composition, and Musicology, as well as MAs in Advanced Musical Studies, and Music Therapy (see the box below).

BRITISH SOCIETY FOR MUSIC THERAPY (BSMT)
A music therapist works with people who find it difficult to communicate verbally. Using instruments as well as the voice the therapist helps these people – either in a group or individually – to find their own 'voice' through music.

For more details, contact the BSMT, which publishes both the *British Journal of Music Therapy* and the *BSMT Bulletin*:
61 Church Hill Road
East Barnet
Herts EN4 8SY
Tel: 020 8441 6226
Website: www.bsmt.org

LOST IN MUSIC

DECIDING WHAT TO STUDY

Which degree course you take will be entirely dependent on where your interests lie. What you must decide is how much of the course you take should be on the practical side and how much on the theoretical side. If your intention is to sing and/or play once you have graduated, then you should opt for a course where a high percentage of your time is spent on instrument or vocal tuition (it pays to find out the names of the professional musicians the college or university employs to teach you). Example degree titles include Professional Musical Theatre National Diploma, Music Composition and Professional Practice, BMus (Hons) Jazz, and BMus (Hons) Music.

You should be aware that because the teaching on these courses is on an intense, often one-to-one basis, you may have to pay for it yourself and so you need to take account of this in your budget. If you are looking to do something other than perform after graduation, an onus on theory might suit you better. Here, the subjects you can study become so diverse almost all interests can be covered. For example you can study Music and Comparative Literature, Music and Psychology, and even Music and Sport Studies. This is why it pays to send off for information and prospectuses early, so you can see what is out there. Where you go and what course you take will influence what it is you actually learn. Below are two examples of course programmes.

ON COURSE 1
At the Royal College of Music, the BMus (Hons) undergraduate programme aims to create professional musicians.

Key Features:

- Study on an instrument related to your principal study (e.g. cor anglais (English horn) alongside oboe).

- Ensemble activities include chamber music coaching by specialist professors.

● Units in professional skills to prepare you for the realities of the music profession (e.g. financial, concert and career planning).

● Units in historical, technical and practical subjects including communication and problem-solving.

● Exchange opportunities with leading international conservatories including Juilliard and Year 3 and 4 students often study in Europe for a term.

Source: The Royal College of Music (RCM)

ON COURSE 2
At the Mountview Theatre Academy you can study for the three year BA (Hons) in Performance with a Musical Theatre option.

Key Features:

● The opportunity to explore and develop a career in performance in theatre and TV, pop, cabaret and session work.

● Students are taught to combine acting, singing and movement in their presentation of a seamless journey of character.

● Within the course equal emphasis is given to the disciplines of singing, dance, movement, voice and acting.

● All students have weekly, one-to-one singing lessons and regular vocal coaching sessions.

● Year 2 students are taught the skills to devise and write a musical.

● Year 3 students concentrate on public performances at Mountview's own venues and other London theatres.

> ● In their final term, students present a West End
> showcase attended by agents, casting directors and
> members of the industry.
>
> Source: Mountview Academy of Theatre Arts

LESS TRADITIONAL OPTIONS

Increasingly, students are looking for colleges where they can study contemporary music, and the jobs surrounding it, in a contemporary setting. Attracting a lot of attention is the BRIT School for Performing Arts and Technology in Croydon. Established 15 years ago and jointly funded by the government and the British Record Industry Trust, it has a state-of-the-art studio, theatre and even its own radio station. The emphasis here is on vocational work and it is the only performing arts school in Britain where entry is free for students between the ages of 14 and 19 years. However, competition for places is fiercer here than almost anywhere else due to the success of former students such as Amy Winehouse and Katie Melua. Each year only 130 14-year-olds and 300 to 350 16-year-olds are taken on and there are often three to four applicants for every place. Selection is based on audition, workshops and interviews and only the most talented get accepted. For more information see Resources.

In Brighton there is the Brighton Institute of Modern Music (BIMM) that opened in 2002 and now has about 350 students spread across its courses. Here, students study guitar, bass, drums or vocals at three levels: Diploma in Modern Music (equivalent to A-level), Higher Diploma (equivalent to the first year of a degree course) and a BA in Professional Musicianship (Diploma and Higher Diploma are accredited by Edexcel, the BA by Sussex University). The emphasis is on performance and on learning about the profession, so all students get the chance to attend masterclasses with the likes of Feeder, Motorhead and Skunk Anansie, while many get to play with name bands while still at the Institute (students have appeared on *Top of the Pops* and have done live shows with the likes of Atomic Kitten and The Sugababes). For more information see Resources.

FASCINATING FACT

Impala (Independent Music Publishers' and Labels' Association) represents more than 2,000 independent (indie) labels across Europe. In the UK, 700 smaller labels account for up to 25 per cent of the UK retail market while the 'big 5' – Universal, Sony, EMI, Warner and BMG – control 74 per cent of the world market.

Source: Impala

MONEY'S TOO TIGHT TO MENTION

FUNDING YOUR TRAINING

As stated previously in the Drama section of this book (Chapters 1–4), at present, students entering higher education in the state system pay up to £3,000 in tuition fees. However, students from lower-income backgrounds can apply for help with this fee and can also apply for student loans to cover living costs (at present the maximum loan is £4,000). For more information on higher education funding, the DfES publishes a guide, *Financial Support For Higher Education Students*, which is available online at www.studentsupportdirect.co.uk. For more information on the DfES, see Resources.

Extremely talented young musicians between the ages of 8 and 18 may be able to get a scholarship under the Music and Dance Scheme (MDS) run by the DfES. This allows them to continue their academic education while getting the best possible music training available. For more information contact the DfES (see Resources).

Non-UCAS (Universities and Colleges Admissions Service) and private schools and colleges can be very expensive but, as in drama, many music colleges and schools offer bursaries and scholarships to the most talented students and you may be able to get sponsorship for your studies. (Full information on how to obtain sponsorship or scholarships is given on page 43.)

FASCINATING FACT

Way back in 1987 the film *Dirty Dancing* made a star out of Patrick Swayze. Now it has been turned into a top-selling West End musical (advance ticket sales were £12 million) and is guaranteed to run until 2008. Coincidentally, the choreographer responsible for all the moves in the film of *Dirty Dancing*, Kenny Ortega, also directed and choreographed *High School Musical*, which recently became the fastest-selling TV film of all time due to phenomenal DVD sales.

CHAPTER 7

I Could Have Danced All Night

DANCING UNCOVERED

Watching the professional dancer plying his or her trade is a visual treat we can all enjoy, be it Darcey Bussell performing classical ballet at the Royal Opera House or young Jamie Bell showing off his more contemporary moves in the film *Billy Elliot*. In fact, the variety of different styles is much wider than you might think and in recent years the world of dance has really opened up with successful shows such as *Tap Dogs*, an all-male *Swan Lake*, *Ballet Boyz* and *Riverdance* bringing dance to a wider audience. Although dance breaks down into three main areas (classical dance, contemporary dance and musical theatre), the range of styles includes ballet, tap, jazz, South Asian, flamenco, tango, salsa, ballroom, African and even break-dancing. You can see dancers in films and theatre shows such as *Chicago* and *Cabaret*, in music videos, in clubs, restaurants and hotels and at large corporate extravaganzas, exhibitions and displays, some even work in the circus such as the performers in Cirque Du Soleil.

FASCINATING FACT

**In 2002 there were 2,300 dance and drama graduates.
Approximately 71 per cent went straight into employment
with around 46 per cent gaining full-time paid work;
16 per cent opted to take further studies.**

Source: HESA

I'M IN THE MOOD FOR DANCING

Not everyone who wants to be a dancer has the necessary skills
or physical attributes to make it. Ballet, in particular, requires
girls to be between 1.52 metres and 1.67 metres tall, while boys
must be between 1.6 metres and 1.78 metres tall. Other dance
forms have less stringent physical requirements, but you will still
need grace and rhythm and the ability to communicate with an
audience through movement to enjoy a successful career. If you
don't have the natural skills and talent to be a professional
dancer yourself but desperately want to work within the dance
sphere, do not despair, there are plenty of other jobs you can do,
some of which you might not even know about. Most of these will
be in the backstage area and include make-up artists, the
wardrobe department and technical crews responsible for the
sound and lighting of shows. You could be a dance journalist or
photographer or a therapist, such as an osteopath, who
specialises in dance injuries. The chart on the next page will show
you just some of the occupations available to people who want to
work in the dance world.

FASCINATING FACT

**The morning of the film shoot for the famous dance scene
in *Singin' in the Rain*, star Gene Kelly woke up with a
raging fever and a cold. Being the perfectionist he was, he
insisted on completing the shoot, even though it meant
dancing in a downpour of rain. The result is one of the
most shown clips in film history.**

JOBS IN DANCE

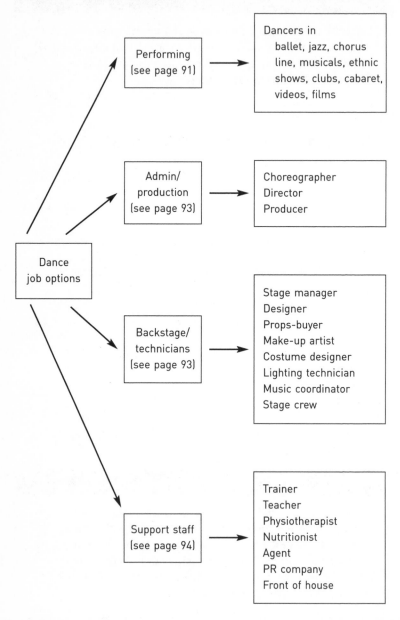

Performing
(see page 91)

Dancers in ballet, jazz, chorus line, musicals, ethnic shows, clubs, cabaret, videos, films

Admin/
production
(see page 93)

Choreographer
Director
Producer

Dance
job options

Backstage/
technicians
(see page 93)

Stage manager
Designer
Props-buyer
Make-up artist
Costume designer
Lighting technician
Music coordinator
Stage crew

Support staff
(see page 94)

Trainer
Teacher
Physiotherapist
Nutritionist
Agent
PR company
Front of house

BEST FOOT FORWARD

As you've probably realised by now, making it as a professional dancer is tough. Because it takes years of physical conditioning, if you haven't actually started training in any form of dance by your mid-teens, it is probably too late to consider becoming a performer seriously. However, if you are already some way along the dancing ladder there are some physical and mental abilities and skills that are really going to help you.

GOOD HEALTH

Dancers are like athletes in that they use their bodies as the tools of their trade. This means they cannot afford ill health and must constantly look after themselves and monitor their fitness. Also, in the same way in which athletes employ the services of sports physiotherapists and trainers, so do dancers. Many dancers participate in yoga and Pilates for body conditioning and regularly visit masseuses, physiotherapists, osteopaths and chiropractors. A dancer's body is like an expensive car – it needs to be finely tuned at all times.

STAMINA

Although actual performances (or a particular dancer's role in them) may only last a few minutes or a couple of hours, this is not the end of the physical story. Dancers have to be constantly at their physical peak. This means they will have regular practice sessions. And the story doesn't end there because they will also have frequent rehearsals for performances. They may be aching from the exertions of the day before, but they still have to put in those hours at the dance studio. It can be physically exhausting and dancers must constantly watch their stamina levels.

DETERMINATION

It may be very early in the morning and freezing outside but the show has to go on which means dancers have still got to rehearse. Endlessly repeating the same sequence of movements for a particular piece may seem mind-numbingly boring but any dancer worth his or her salt will be determined to get it right, not just because customers pay good money to watch performances, but because if you are performing in an ensemble one dancer's mistake could throw out the performances of everyone else on stage.

ATTENTION TO DETAIL

Although as a spectator you may not always see the complexity and precision of every movement on stage, the dancer most definitely does. He or she will know when a hand is at the wrong angle, or a foot is in the wrong place, and the best dancers are those who are not satisfied with nearly right, but with perfection. This constant need to be better at what they do marks out really good dancers from the mediocre (see Celia Grannum's case study on pages 96–7).

GOOD SPATIAL MEMORY

Your spatial memory helps you remember where your arm or leg is in relation to the space around you. Dancers use their spatial memories to learn their dance steps, so they can remember how high they should hold their arms and which movement follows which within a dance piece. Dancers memorising choreography is a bit like actors learning their lines, except for the dancer the whole body is involved. If you have a good spatial memory it will help you to learn new routines quickly, ensuring that rehearsals go much more smoothly.

CONCENTRATION

Closely aligned to spatial memory is concentration, because the harder you concentrate on what you are doing, the more quickly you can master it. Some dance pieces may not be very long, but they can contain hundreds of precise movements, some of which have to be executed at speed, so if you don't concentrate you could end up in a knotted pile in the corner. You have to sustain your concentration until the end of the piece and this is even more important when dancing as part of a corps de ballet or in a chorus line where lots of people are on stage at the same time. If you end up facing the wrong way in the wrong place, you can put out the placements for the whole of the group. If you are a male dancer lifting a dancing partner, concentration is crucial because one slip could lead to a serious injury.

PASSION

It may sound corny, but you really do need a passion for what you do to make it in dance. This is because there will always be someone out there hungrier, who wants it more than you, and when it comes to getting jobs it is the hungry dancer who gets the fattest worms! Dancing jobs are at a premium and no one wants to watch a mediocre dancer who can't really be bothered to put in the effort. A passionate dancer will receive the best job offers and the biggest accolades each and every time.

ALL THAT JAZZ

If all of the above are going to help you make it in the world of dance, then there are some mental and physical attributes that could seriously hold you back. Check the list below to see whether a career in dancing is a viable option for you.

PHYSICAL PROBLEMS

Most of us would love to imagine ourselves moving effortlessly and gracefully along to a musical rhythm; unfortunately for many it remains a dream as they seem to have been born with two left feet. If you suffer from a lack of coordination or from extreme clumsiness (known as dyspraxia), mastering complex dance moves is going to be difficult. If you have a physical disability, opportunities to work within the dance arena will be limited, although some dance troupes have actually turned this into their own unique selling point. CandoCo is a contemporary dance group that contains both able-bodied and disabled dancers and runs training courses for the disabled (for more details see Resources). Physical problems obviously include injuries, many of which are caused by dancers lifting other dancers. This is why the most common injuries in men involve back problems, while in female dancers it is the hips that suffer the most. The most common physical problem of all though is arthritis, where the joints become inflamed because of overuse and overstretching. Such problems can shorten a dancer's career quite considerably.

FASCINATING FACT

During the teen years both boys and girls put on a growth spurt. This distorts the body's own spatial memory of itself and it takes a little while to get used to having longer legs and arms. This leaves many teenagers permanently tired (from all that growing) and extremely clumsy and accident-prone. During this time certain dance exercises they could once perform easily become almost impossible for them. However, once the spurt slows down and the body 'recognises' its new size they soon find their old physical prowess returning.

CAREER LONGEVITY

A dancing career is almost certainly not going to last you for life, so you will have to come to terms with the fact that your days on stage are numbered. Most dancers accept this and make provision for life after dancing by establishing themselves as a dance teacher or by having another skill, such as becoming a physical therapist of some sort (yoga or Pilates teacher, physical conditioning practitioner or nutritionist). However, if the thought of having to change careers while friends outside the industry are just beginning to establish themselves in theirs fills you with dread, maybe you should consider another career from the outset.

HEIGHT

Ideas about the way dancers should look may be slowly (ever so slowly) changing, but there is a good reason why dancers (especially ballet dancers) have traditionally been of modest height. It's because when dancing duets they will frequently be lifted by their partner and the smaller you are the easier you are to lift. There is also an aesthetic aspect to it, because the visual contrast of a muscular male dancer with his petite female partner is seen as very pleasing. Many companies want the dancers in their corps de ballet or chorus line to be the same height because it gives visual symmetry when they are on stage. If you are tall your height may count against you. However, more contemporary or non-western dance may suit you better. In fact, the famous Bluebell Girls from Paris's Moulin Rouge (home of the cancan) all have to be over six foot in height!

WEIGHT

Dancers and their weight is a very serious issue. If you are overweight you may find it difficult to compete in the job market against other dancers with slimmer figures. Once again, if a male dancer is going to be lifting you, then the smaller you are the easier his job becomes. However, the obsession with body shape and size within the dance community is one the industry itself is addressing. This is because so many dancers suffer from eating disorders. Sad to say, but there are still some dance companies where dancers are encouraged to be as skinny as possible. In order to get skinny and stay skinny some dancers will starve themselves, leading to all sorts of physical problems both in the short and long term. Dance UK is the national development agency for dance and is well aware of the situation. In response it has produced the Healthier Dance Programme giving advice on health and nutrition (see Resources for more information).

ATTENTION DEFICIT/LACK OF DISCIPLINE
If your mind keeps wandering off the job in hand you are never going to make it as a dancer where pinpoint timing is sometimes the only thing between you and crashing into the audience. Non-stop practice trains your body to follow the choreography but it is up to you to keep your mind on track. You have to be disciplined, not just about the dancing practice but also about your diet and lifestyle – if you have an important performance coming up you can't afford to spend hours partying with friends. If you think you may lack the discipline to be tucked up in bed early while others are out enjoying themselves, you may have to think again about a career in dance.

SUSCEPTIBILITY TO STRESS
Some people find they really can't hack it as dancers because they just cannot cope with performance stress. 'Stage fright' can afflict the most seasoned professional but most find some kind of coping mechanism (which is why so many of them practise yoga or meditation). If you are simply paralysed by nerves each and every time you go to dance in front of an audience, you may like to consider some other job within the dance area otherwise you could end up with a serious stress-related illness.

ANTISOCIAL HOURS
As in the worlds of drama and music, most dance performances will take place in the evenings and at weekends when the audience can get away from its own work. This means dancers may spend many hours in rehearsal or at dance class during the day and then find themselves working on stage at night. You may also go off on tour with your dance company meaning your hours become even more irregular (think of the travel involved). Not only the performers work antisocial hours, but also the technical people involved in putting on dance shows. If you are looking for a typical 9am to 5pm day, you may like to consider other areas of employment in the industry.

FASCINATING FACT

Proving the exception to the rule, the great Latvian ballet dancer Mikhail Baryshnikov is still performing in public at the age of 59. In 2006 he performed in the USA and Spain with Hell's Kitchen Dance.

SPOTLIGHT ON LONDON CHILDREN'S BALLET (LCB)
Set up in 1994 the London Children's Ballet is a non-profit-making organisation which aims to help children from all walks of life to achieve their dreams whatever their ability, size or shape. Each year, more than 600 children aged between 9 and 14 years audition to secure one of the 50 places on the scheme and rehearse for six months before performing live. Two performances are given for charities and schools where tickets cost just £1 each. It is estimated over 10,000 people have seen their first ballet via LCB. LCB2 is an outreach project of LCB, which takes ballet to special needs schools and care homes in Greater London, so those who cannot visit a theatre can also experience live dance.

Source: www.londonchildrensballet.com

CHAPTER 8

Dancing Queens (and Kings)

'Dancing, for me, is almost a spiritual experience.'
Celia Grannum, freelance professional dancer

The chart on page 84 will have given you some idea of what career opportunities actually exist in dance and here we will explore what each job within the industry entails.

PERFORMING

The opportunities for dancers have increased dramatically in the last 20 years. For a start, more people than ever are taking dance classes – everything from ceroc to salsa – and this has increased their interest in seeing live dance as entertainment. Where once dance was viewed as being quite elitist, mainly because classical ballet was the only live dance form you could actually go to see and was horrendously expensive, new shows like *Lord of the Dance* and renewed interest in flamenco and tango have brought a new, younger and trendier audience to dance. This renewed interest means more dance shows, which means more dancers.

Also, the dance club culture of the 1990s has increased dance's exposure on TV, film and video.

DANCE IN FILM

In the 1970s, John Travolta became famous for his dance moves in *Saturday Night Fever*, which led to the explosion of the disco craze across the world. Dancing is still popular in films today, such as the Hollywood blockbusters *Chicago*, *Moulin Rouge* and Disney's *High School Musical*.

In 2004 the film *Honey*, starring Jessica Alba of TV's *Dark Angel*, was released in Britain. Alba plays a young New York dancer and choreographer who gets her big break choreographing the dance routines for music videos by the likes of Missy Elliott and Ginuwine. The film was directed by Bille Woodruff, who has directed videos for Britney Spears and Usher. Choreography was by Laurieann Gibson who has worked with P. Diddy, Mary J. Blige and Brandy.

Dancers now work for established dance companies like Rambert Dance Company and the Royal Ballet; they work as session dancers for TV shows and for videos; they work live on stage in musical theatre; they work in nightclubs and in cabaret, and some even put on the floor shows in holiday camps and on cruise liners. Some specialise in classical ballet, others in one or more areas of contemporary dance, still others (like Joaquin Cortes) have only one speciality (flamenco).

THE LIFE OF A PERFORMER

A dancer's life is a demanding one, with hours of practice and rehearsals to get through as well as performance stress and the physical stress of demanding 100 per cent from your body on a daily basis. They must watch out for injury and keep up to date with the latest dance trends and moves, which entails taking lots of dance classes. Many dancers go on tour and all that travelling can bring its own demands and problems.

Most dancers tend to be freelance and go from job to job and contract to contract and, just like actors and musicians, dancers expect to spend some time out of work; that is why it is so important for them to have other skills they can use for alternative employment (e.g. dance teacher).

ADMINISTRATION/PRODUCTION

Many dancers go on to do their own choreography; in fact many choreographers are very talented dancers in their own right (Britain's Michael Clark for one). The choreographer's job is to come up with the dance moves the dancers then follow – he or she is a bit like a musical composer, but they use movements instead of notes. You need a sound technical knowledge of dance for this job and for many dancers this is their preferred career route when they retire from active dancing themselves. While the choreographer concentrates on what the dancers are doing, the director of a dance show is intent on getting all the elements – lighting, dancing, costume, music – coming together and being right on the night (a bit like a conductor), while the producer has to make sure everything goes to budget and that the costs do not over-run astronomically.

Dance notation is the art of writing dance movements down, a bit like a composer notating music and, as in music, there are now specific computer software packages to make the task of notating easier. This is a pretty specialised job and you need to have a genuine passion for dance to have an interest in notation.

BACKSTAGE/TECHNICIANS

As in all areas where live performance or televised/filmed performance is concerned, the technical staff are essential. This becomes especially true with live dance, where safety concerns are paramount. Set designers must ensure their artistic visions don't endanger the dancers. No one wants to see the sugarplum fairy fall over a piece of scenery. Likewise, the costume designer must ensure the dancers can actually move in their outfits.

Although the Royal Ballet can mount very extravagant productions, many contemporary companies actually use very pared-down sets and costumes, but this is not true of all areas in dance. As we saw in the Drama section of this book (Chapters 1–4), musical theatre is hugely popular in Britain and although these are not pure dance shows, many contain dance numbers. Audiences pay large sums to see the stunning visual effects and props in shows such as *Les Miserables*, *Chitty Chitty Bang Bang* and *Miss Saigon* and so the input of lighting and sound technicians, prop-makers and special-effects teams is invaluable. Other areas backstage you might like to consider are make-up, wig-maker and wardrobe.

SUPPORT STAFF

Like actors, many established dancers are members of Equity and have their own agents. The agent will inform their client about auditions and new shows coming up, and will generally promote their talents. Larger dance companies will have their own PR departments to liaise with TV and print journalists about forthcoming shows and guest star appearances. In fact, you could decide to become a dance journalist, reviewing live dance performances and reporting on dance news stories. One recent trend in dance has been the expansion of the community dance sector. The community dance worker may operate in conjunction with social services or the local education authority to help people of all ages and of all abilities to communicate through movement and dance.

The dance therapist has a similar role but will normally be working with people who have problems expressing their feelings and emotions through verbal communication. However, the most important members of support staff for a dancer are those that oversee their physical welfare. Many dancers become dance teachers whose role is not only vital for the education of young dancers coming into the system, but also for the established dancers who must keep practising on a daily basis.

Also essential are the physiotherapists, osteopaths, chiropractors and other physical therapists that help the dancer to overcome injury and the physical stresses that dancing puts on the body. Many established companies employ their own physical therapists but most freelance dancers must pay for this themselves. Equity now offers dance members a special insurance scheme in case of injury.

FASCINATING FACT

In January 2006, the winners of the 2005 Critics' Circle National Dance Awards were announced at the Royal Opera House in London. The stars of dance were splendidly represented with classical ballet's ballerinas Dame Beryl Grey (National Dance Awards Patron), Darcey Bussell (Principal Dancer, The Royal Ballet) and Zoë Ball and her *Strictly Come Dancing* partner Ian Waite, applauding as the winners were announced. The afternoon was a special triumph for the Royal Ballet, which frequently performs at the Royal Opera House: in total, the company scooped no fewer than three of the major awards, for Outstanding Repertoire (classical), Best Choreography (classical) and Best Female Dancer.

Picking up the coveted prizes for Best Male and Best Female Dancer were Thomas Lund of the Royal Danish Ballet and Marianela Nunez of the Royal Ballet, while the awards for Outstanding Artist went to Maidenhead-born Rupert Pennefather in the classical section, and Akram Khan in the modern. Pennefather recently partnered Darcey Bussell in Frederick Ashton's ballet *A Month in the Country*, while Khan's ground-breaking dance company has recently been working in Hungary and the Netherlands. *Billy Elliot* choreographer Peter Darling collected the award for Best Choreography in a piece of musical theatre.

Guests at the event included the Cuban superstar Carlos Acosta, the newly appointed director of English National Ballet Wayne Eagling, Lady Deborah MacMillan, choreographer Arlene Phillips, TV star Jeremy Sheffield and the actor and dancer Adam Garcia.

Source: Critics' Circle, Dance Branch,
www.nationaldanceawards.com

CELIA GRANNUM, 29, FREELANCE DANCER/
DANCE TEACHER/PILATES TEACHER

Celia is originally from Barbados and trained at the Tisch School of the Arts, a part of New York University in America. When she first came to England she worked as a dance teacher at a boarding school in Surrey and is now involved with Exchange Music and Dance Company, and Ballet Black.

'I've always had multiple interests and when you are freelancing you really need them because there will be times when you are not working. I still teach dance at the boarding school in Surrey and I also teach Pilates, so those give me a regular income. I have a friend who has done some dancing for a major pop star, and jobs like that are great because you get paid substantial sums and you can save them to tide you over during the lean times. I did a job for Iron Maiden for their single 'Rainmaker' where I had to wear a grass skirt and be covered in mud and be soaked all day and I got paid a measly £250 for that! But I love to dance. For me it is almost a spiritual experience. When I'm dancing it is almost as if I'm not here, I go somewhere else. It's the physicality of it, moving and feeling free in your body. It's a joy and an exhilaration and it's all about communicating with your audience.

'Injury is a serious consideration for anybody who is working with their body. At Ballet Black we get free physical therapy, but freelance dancers usually have to pay for it themselves and it can get very expensive. I have a recurring ankle injury and I am considering having an operation but I'm doing a lot of dance work at the moment so it's about finding the right time to do it.

'The other thing that is dangerous about dancing, apart from the physical, is the mental injury. If you do the more traditional styles of dance such as ballet you are always aiming for a physical ideal and you can get to a place in your head where you believe you are never good enough. If you keep telling yourself that every day then it becomes a self-fulfilling prophecy – you never will be good enough – and that wears away at your self-confidence. There's also the problem of weight. I've personally never had a weight problem but it can get to be so depending on whom you work for. Some companies do like their dancers to be extremely thin. You really have to watch out for that because it can make you paranoid and some dancers do end up starving themselves.

'I'd say to anyone out there considering this as a career to just follow their heart and don't be swayed. There are a lot of negatives attached to it but give it a shot and if it isn't for you then that's fine. Dancing is one of those things where you can't wait until later to get into it. So if you are 15 or 16 years old and have that burning desire to be a dancer, try it out now because it is better to discover it's not working out now than to look back at the age of 40 and realise you can no longer give it a try because physically it's just too late.'

JOYCE AMBROSE, 26, PGCE TRAINEE DANCE TEACHER

Joyce studied for her BTEC National (equivalent to 2 A-levels) in Singing, Acting and Dancing and also did A-level Dancing before auditioning to Liverpool John Moores University, to do a degree in Dance/Drama. As she is dyslexic, the university suggested she would do better just on the Dance course, which she subsequently did. She graduated in 2002 and took a year out to travel before starting her PGCE, also at John Moores.

'The degree course I did involved lots of dance in the community and the university said my social skills were so good that teaching would suit me as I wanted to work with people with disabilities and also with children. On the PGCE you have a teaching place three days a week in a school and two days in university and after half term in February this year, it will be five days a week in the school teaching just dance. You go into school as a dance specialist; basically you do your PGCE under Physical Education (PE) with a lot of PE students, so my actual PGCE will say PE (Dance). I do hip hop, street dance, break-dancing, jazz, contemporary or modern but I don't really do that much ballet. I tend to do a lot of street dance in school to get the boys involved because they tend to think that dance is girlie – "Boys don't do dance, dancing is for girls" – and I always ask them about break-dancing and teach them to do the caterpillar and the windmill.

'I do a lot of dance for myself as well. There's a place called Merseyside Dance Initiative in Liverpool and I do a lot of dance classes there because when you are a dance teacher it is very hard to actually get to do any dance yourself. You go in, warm up, show the class a routine, but you don't actually dance and from the performing side of it you get such a buzz. It's not that I don't get a buzz out of teaching, I leave after teaching on a high, but it is a very different feeling from performing. I do a contemporary class, a street-dance class and a break-dance class so I can see what's going on and what new moves are coming through. I don't always get to do them every week but I do as much as I can because it also helps me keep up with the music.

'Of course I would like to be a performer, but you look at what they have to be, they have to be a certain weight and a certain height and look a certain way and if you are not what they are looking for you get rejected and that can really hurt. I wouldn't want to put myself through that.

'I didn't start dancing until I was 15 years old when I went to a jazz class and when I got to university everyone had done ballet and I hadn't. So for six months I tried to teach myself as much as I could and I trained my body and I worked really hard because I believe you need to be passionate about what you are doing. Teaching dance may not be my first passion, dancing is, but it still has something to do with what I want to do and I know I'm good at it. You also have to be competitive – you can't help but judge yourself.

'You do need to have people skills to become a teacher. It's no good if you are timid in front of a class because the kids will suss you out. You also have to be authoritative and show them who's boss. You also need to know your subject, because they will always ask you the question you don't know the answer to! You can't expect your pupils to respect your subject if you don't respect it yourself. You will never ever be able to encourage other people to go on to do your subject. If you think dance has got value, and I do think it has, then your pupils will think it has value too. I do believe I am making a difference. I want to inspire my pupils.'

FASCINATING FACT

33-year-old Christopher Wheeldon, one-time choreographer with the New York City Ballet, has decided to set up a new dance company called Morphoses. Wheeldon says he has been inspired by the Ballets Russes created by Diaghilev in 1909. Morphoses will have a permanent home at Sadler's Wells in London as well as a site in New York. The permanent company is to be launched in 2008 but there will be some performances in 2007 featuring some of the best dancers in the world.

CHAPTER 9

A World in Motion

'Be passionate about what you are doing because I think once you lose your passion, there is no point doing it. I still get excited about dancing, I really do.'
Joyce Ambrose, Trainee Dance Teacher

SHOW ME THE MONEY

Dancing with Beyonce may sound incredibly exciting, however it may not make you rich. Although it's true that big corporate affairs do tend to pay more than everyday dance events (they tend to have bigger budgets), they don't come along every week. In fact, most dancers, especially those in the corps de ballet or in the chorus line, get modest wages; it is only when you become a star or a known-name that the money becomes substantial. Equity negotiates the minimum wages for dancers in the UK and for a ballet dance artiste it is approximately £304 a week. A junior member of a corps de ballet earns between £14,000 and £17,500, while a soloist earns £22,000 and a principal earns £30,400. In contemporary dance the wages tend to be lower than in classical dance. Choreographers should earn a minimum of £536 a week or £998 on tours or seasons.

TRANSFERABLE SKILLS

As in all areas of the performing arts, dancers can expect to have periods of unemployment and so should definitely acquire other skills. Many go into teaching (if you want to teach in a state school you will have to obtain a PGCE), especially as so many members of the public now take dance classes, and many study privately to become therapists in disciplines associated with keeping the body fit and healthy (masseuse, reflexologist or Pilates teacher). The one thing all dancers should bear in mind is that their performing career will be relatively short and so they should formulate a long-term career plan that they intend to follow once their dancing days are over. Many go into arts administration, choreography and dance therapy.

DANCE CLASS

If you really believe you have what it takes to be a professional dancer then there are some things you should be doing already to increase your chances of success:

- If you have not started taking **dance classes** by your early teens you really need to start doing so now. This is especially true if you want to be a classical dancer. For ballet, girls need to start *at the very latest* by the age of 12, and boys by 14. You should be taking graded examinations (e.g. the Royal Academy of Dancing, RAD). There are almost no opportunities for an adult in dance training.

- **Stay flexible**. This is true both physically and mentally. You need to keep yourself fit and healthy but you should also flex your mind by going to see as many dance performances as possible, in as many styles. Check out flamenco as well as ballet, and street dance as well as contemporary.

- **Know your history**. If you can show a real love and knowledge of your subject it will give you an advantage over other candidates. There are plenty of books, videos and DVDs that will help you track the history of dance.

- **Practise!** Dance is a demanding discipline and if you start to let things slide it will show. They say 'practice makes perfect', and in dance the need to practise is paramount. If you don't have the passion and the motivation to practise regularly, you may like to consider doing something else within the dance arena.

● One of the best things you can do to show you really are committed to a career in dance is to take a vocational **qualification** such as a BTEC National Diploma or GNVQ (S/NVQ) in Performing Arts (Dance). Taken from the age of 16 this is a very popular way to prepare yourself for higher education in dance. Contact Creative and Cultural Skills and Skillset for more information (see Resources).

WHERE TO GO? WHAT TO DO?

Although academic qualifications are not mandatory, to get onto a dance course you will normally have to pass an audition (you may have to pay an audition fee), have an interview and in some cases a medical examination to assess your spatial awareness and physical articulation. Degree courses, however, normally have an entrance minimum of five GCSEs and two A-levels, or three Scottish Highers plus equivalent.

Before applying for any course however, you should be thinking about what you want to do once you have finished training. If you want to enter the West End or do chorus-line work, a course at a musical theatre school where you train in a multitude of disciplines including acting, singing and jazz dance will be most appropriate. If contemporary dance is your forte then contemporary dance schools such as the London Contemporary Dance School offer thorough training in a variety of contemporary styles and techniques such as Cunningham or Graham, and usually include ballet as a main course subject. However, these courses are very expensive and places are much sought after.

Finally, if you are serious about becoming a ballet dancer, you should already be well into your training. The Music and Dance Scheme (MDS) funds children and young people between the ages of 11 and 18 to receive an academic education alongside specialist music and ballet training. Four dance schools offer MDS places to students at 11 years old: the Royal Ballet School, Elmhurst School For Dance and Performing Arts, The Hammond School, and Arts Educational School, Tring Park (for more information contact the Council for Dance Education and Training (CDET), see Resources). Ballet training is very intensive and entry onto courses is strictly limited to those with exceptional skills and talent.

If you want to study dance on a more academic level, then a degree course at university might suit you. This will involve a certain amount of vocational training but will also cover theory, history, choreography and other subjects.

ON COURSE
A dance degree at university may include a number of the following topics:

- Directing

- Dance in the community

- Choreography

- Dance in education

- Mime/ballet

- Contemporary dance

- Performance

- History of dance

- Performance analysis.

Source: *CRAC Degree Course Guides 2003/4:
Music, Drama and Dance*, published by Trotman

However, if you really, really want to dance as a performer you should be looking for a place at a specialist dance school. Courses here tend to be of three years' duration. They usually lead to a degree or a diploma and will involve many hours each day in practical work. The Council for Dance Education and Training (CDET) accredits the following dance courses and they are inspected by government agencies as well as the CDET. All qualifications are awarded by Trinity College, London and you may be eligible for funding (see pages 106–7).

SCHOOL	COURSE/S	TYPE OF FUNDING
Arts Ed London	Musical Theatre Course 3 yr	DaDA*
Arts Educational School, Tring Park	Dance Course 2 yr	DaDA
Bird College	BA (Hons) Dance & Theatre 2 yr	DaDA
	Musical Theatre Course 3 yr	DaDA
Bodywork Dance Studio	Professional Dance Course 3 yr	DaDA
	Musical Theatre Course 3 yr (not CDET accredited)	DaDA
Central School of Ballet	Classical Ballet 2 yr	DaDA
	Professional Performers 3 yr	Full Fees
	BA (Hons) Professional Dance 3 yr	DaDA
Elmhurst	Classical Ballet Course 3 yr	DaDA
English National Ballet School	Intensive Classical Ballet Course 2 yr (not CDET accredited)	DaDA
The Hammond School	National Diploma in Professional Dance 3 yr	DaDA

SCHOOL	COURSE/S	TYPE OF FUNDING
Italia Conti Academy	Performing Arts Course 3 yr	DaDA
Laban Centre	BA (Hons) Dance Theatre Course 3 yr	Full Fees
	Professional Diploma in Dance Studies 1 yr	Full Fees
	Professional Diploma Community Dance 1 yr	State-Funded HE
Laine Theatre Arts	Musical Theatre Performers & Teachers Course 3 yr	DaDA
Liverpool Theatre School	Musical Theatre Course 3 yr (not CDET accredited)	DaDA
London Contemporary Dance School	One year Certificate I yr	State-Funded HE
	BA (Hons) Contemporary Dance 3 yr	State-Funded HE
London Studio Centre	BA (Hons) Theatre Dance 3 yr	State-Funded HE
	Diploma (HE) Theatre Dance 3 yr	State-Funded HE
Merseyside Dance & Drama Centre	Teacher & Performance Course Dance 3 yr	Full Fees
	Musical Theatre 3 yr (not CDET accredited)	Full Fees
Midlands Academy of Dance & Drama	Musical Theatre Course 3 yr (not CDET accredited)	Full Fees
Millennium Dance 2000	Professional Diploma in Performance 3 yr (not CDET accredited)	DaDA
Northern Ballet School	Professional Dancer's Course 3 yr	DaDA
	Dance Teacher's Diploma Course 3 yr	DaDA

SCHOOL	COURSE/S	TYPE OF FUNDING
Northern School of Contemporary Dance	BA in Performance Arts (Dance) 3 yr	State-Funded HE
	Graduate Diploma in Dance 1 yr (not CDET accredited)	State-Funded HE
Performers' College	Performers Theatre Dance Course 3 yr	DaDA
Rambert School	BA (Hons) Ballet & Contemporary Dance 3 yr	DaDA
	Advance Professional Certificate 1 yr	Full Fees
Royal Academy of Dance	BA (Hons) Ballet Education 3 yr	State-Funded HE
	BA (Hons) Dance Education 3 yr	Full Fees
Royal Ballet School	11 Plus Course 5 yr	MDS[†]
	Dancer's Course 3 yr (not CDET accredited)	MDS
Stella Mann College	Professional Dance Course 3 yr	DaDA
	Musical Theatre Course 3 yr	DaDA
SLP College	Professional Musical Theatre	DaDA
Urdang Academy	Performers Diploma 3 yr	DaDA

*DaDA stands for Dance and Drama Awards
[†]MDS stands for Music and Dance Scheme

Source: Council for Dance Education and Training

MONEY MATTERS

As previously mentioned, the Music and Dance Scheme (MDS) funds young people between the ages of 11 and 18 to train for a career in ballet. Funding is income related, so the amount received will depend on the income of parents or guardians. Contact the Department for Education and Skills (DfES) for more information (see Resources).

STATE-FUNDED HE COURSES

On these courses, students pay up to £3,000 a year tuition fees but if you come from a low-income background you can apply for help. You can also apply for a student loan for help in covering the cost of travel, accommodation, etc. For more information, contact the DfES information line: 08456 077 577.

DANCE AND DRAMA AWARDS (DaDA)

Introduced in 1999, these awards help with fees and maintenance for talented students wishing to go into dance. Courses eligible for DaDA funding can be one, two or three years in duration. Your financial circumstances may be taken into account when an award is given, but this is only secondary to your talent. Only 60 per cent of students on a particular course will be provided with DaDAs, the rest will have to fund their own places.

FULL FEES OR INDEPENDENT COURSES

Vocational training in dance does not come cheap; this is because classes are often small or the training is provided on a one-to-one basis. Courses that do not attract funding from the state sector can cost upwards of £10,000 per year. However, you may still be able to find financial help in the form of a scholarship or bursary. Many dance schools have funds specifically aimed at talented students who need help in covering course fees. For these you must enquire direct to the dance schools. It is also possible to raise funds through sponsorship and through charities, trusts and foundations. All these forms of funding are covered in more detail on page 43.

CHAPTER 10

Opportunity Knocks

THE FACE OF PERFORMING ARTS

For many years the performing arts did not reflect the rich racial mix of our society. This was truer in the drama and dance areas than in contemporary music where the influence of African, or more importantly, Afro-American culture was crucial to the development of jazz, the blues, soul music, and eventually hip hop and rap. Because of this there were many black musicians in the public eye, however there were very few black or Asian actors or dancers seen in our theatres, in films or on our TV screens – and if they did appear it was normally in a stereotypical role.

The situation over the past few years has changed quite rapidly, mainly because as society has become more racially integrated, more ethnic writers, directors, actors and dancers have brought their productions and performances to our stages and screens. Oscar wins for Denzel Washington and Halle Berry, starring roles for British actors such as Parminder Nagra in *Bend It Like Beckham* and *ER*, and Adrian Lester's magnificent performance as Henry V at the National Theatre and in the TV series *Hustle*, have increased our awareness of black and Asian actors. There are now many ethnic dance groups such as Adzido and Akademi. However, in January 2004 an Iranian born actor, 33-year-old Alan Marni, decided to sue his agency after being told he should forget about playing Shakespeare and go for roles as a terrorist or shopkeeper. Mr Marni is thought to be the first actor to sue his agency over discrimination.

SUPPORTING MINORITY GROUPS

CC Skills, the Sector Skills Council for the arts and entertainment industry, is committed to supporting equal employment opportunities for everybody regardless of their ethnic group, gender or physical ability. However, the truth very much remains that the arts are still predominated by people who are white. According to research carried out by CC Skills, 94.7 per cent of people who work in the arts are white, while only 0.9 per cent are Asian or British Asian, and 0.9 per cent are Black or British Black. Overall, 54 per cent of people who work in the sector are male, while 46 per cent are female. People with disabilities are still under-represented in all areas of the performing arts, although the CanDoCo contemporary dance company does run workshops for both able-bodied and disabled people (see Resources), and although many performers are of ethnic origin, it is still rare to see a black or Asian person backstage.

Meanwhile, the business and technical sides of the music scene are still dominated by men. Much of this is down to traditional perceptions of what men and women do – females in secretarial roles and men doing technical jobs (it's why they are known as 'the backroom boys') – and what areas of work people of ethnic origins have traditionally been employed in.

Tania Peach, the production manager at Mountview Academy is well aware of the problem:

'We only have one black student (on the technical side) here at Mountview and I am convinced it is to do with role models and that will not change until we, the people on the training side, start to change it. From the stage management and technical point of view there is nothing prohibitive at all, anyone can do this, whatever sex or race they are. Another way we can change things is through our community workshops where we can reach people who would not normally come into contact with the theatre or the dramatic arts.'

Below is the experience of one Asian actor in the theatre and on film and TV over the past 20 years.

AMERJIT DEU, ACTOR

Amerjit's family is originally from India but he was raised in Leeds before attending the Douglas Webber Academy of Dramatic Art in London. Over the last 20 years he has worked on stage, in TV (he played Dr Singh in *EastEnders*) and in films (he appeared in *Bend It Like Beckham*) and has seen attitudes to actors of ethnic origin slowly change.

'Although I have seen things change incredibly, I think discrimination is still there, but hidden. For example, when I did *EastEnders*, I remember asking the producers for various things that I knew the white actors on the set got, but I didn't. Asian actors still do tend to get typecast, but that applies more to older Asian actors than the younger actors. As an Asian you are still pigeonholed. Especially on British television we are seen as doctors, lawyers or cornershop owners! As an actor I do sometimes feel that casting directors should have more creative input because for a long time they have been scared. If it says in the script a young, middle-class couple in London, they tend to go for a white couple, while what they should say is "OK, why don't we go for a black or Asian couple?"

'At the moment there are far more parts for young Asian and black actors. The TV show *Holby City* is fantastic as far as representing loads of ethnic backgrounds. There's a black nurse, a black surgeon, an Asian doctor and the patients are a total ethnic mix, just as it would be in a real hospital. However, *Coronation Street* hasn't really caught up with that yet, it is still very white.

'Shows like *The Kumars at No. 42* and *Goodness Gracious Me* have really helped our cause though because they have shown the majority of white, middle-class directors that Asian actors can play different roles, not just shopkeepers or accountants! I think the opportunities for young Asian and

black people working in the performing arts are just
going to get better and better. There will be more writers,
directors and producers out there who come from
multi-ethnic backgrounds and so it will make sense for
them to be writing multi-ethnic parts and directing ethnic
actors in those parts. There are more parts now for young
Asian and black actors than there have ever been.'

CHAPTER 11

The Final Word

Once you have finally trained and entered the real world of the performing arts you will very soon discover getting work is far from easy. If you have attended an accredited course that gives you automatic membership of either Equity or the Musicians' Union, then you will be at an advantage because prospective employers will consider you to be professionally minded. However, you will still have to audition and below are some pointers for getting that elusive job:

- Get yourself a professionally shot **showreel or promotional photographs**. These are not cheap but they may be a way of getting your foot in the door with casting directors.

- Get yourself an **agent**. Once again it will make you look professional and they may have access to audition information that you don't.

- Scour the industry **publications and websites** for news on jobs/shows/new companies being formed (see Resources for a comprehensive list).

- **Be a good networker**. Sometimes word of mouth can be the best way to find out about jobs.

- If you want to be a film-maker then **shoot a short film** or get involved with one by offering to be a runner, do hair and make-up, scout locations or just make the tea. The short-film format is increasingly becoming the way up-and-coming directors get noticed – after winning an Oscar for her short film *Wasp*, director Andrea Arnold shot her first feature *Red Road* which went on to win the Jury Prize at the Cannes Film Festival. If you are interested in learning more about short films visit the Futureshorts website at www.futureshorts.com.

- **Don't give up!** Performers have to take the psychological bumps when they are unsuccessful at auditions. Put it behind you and concentrate on the next job and the next audition.

- **Take extra classes**, learn new skills and concentrate on Continuing Professional Development (CPD). The performing arts don't stand still so nor should you.

- **Know your lines/notes/dance steps**. It cannot be emphasised enough that a professional attitude will get you work and keep you in work so practise and be prepared. This includes doing your homework on what the job is, who it is for, and how long it will last.

- **Smile.** Remember you are selling yourself, so smile, be personable, be interested and keep telling yourself that you are going to get that job – and you will!

The performing arts are currently thriving in Great Britain, mainly due to the fact we have more leisure time and disposable income than ever before and, being sociable by nature, we want to be entertained! That means going to the cinema, visiting the theatre, watching dance performances and listening to music. If you truly believe you have the considerable skills and talents it takes to make it in this extremely competitive world you will enjoy the added bonus of knowing you have a job doing what you love.

GOOD LUCK! Or should that be **BREAK A LEG!**

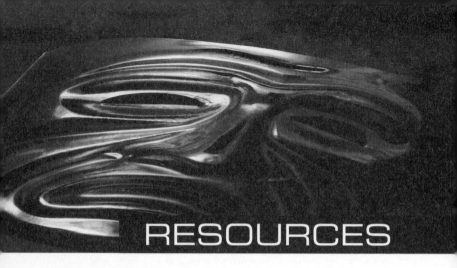

FEATURED SCHOOLS AND COLLEGES

BRIGHTON INSTITUTE OF MODERN MUSIC (BIMM)
7 Rock Place
Brighton BN2 1PF
Website: www.bimm.co.uk
Tel: 01273 626666

BRIT SCHOOL FOR PERFORMING ARTS AND TECHNOLOGY (BRIT)
60 The Crescent
Croydon CR0 2HN
Tel: 020 8665 5242
Website: www.brit.croydon.sch.uk

CAN*DO*CO
Can*do*Co dance company provides workshops for both able-bodied and disabled people.
2T Leroy House
436 Essex Road
London N1 3QP
Tel: 020 7704 6845
Website: www.candoco.co.uk
Email: info@candoco.co.uk

MOUNTVIEW ACADEMY OF THEATRE ARTS
Mountview offers courses in acting, directing and technical theatre. It has an excellent reputation with masterclasses provided

by the likes of Lynn Redgrave and Mike Leigh. Former students include Amanda Holden.

Ralph Richardson Memorial Studios
Clarendon Road
Wood Green
London N22 6XF
Tel: 020 8881 2201
Website: www.mountview.ac.uk
Email: enquiries@mountview.ac.uk

NATIONAL FILM AND TELEVISION SCHOOL
Established in 1970, it is the most highly regarded film school in the country. The school functions as a postgraduate course so most students are slightly older than the average and many have already had some employment in the industry.

Beaconsfield Studios
Station Road
Beaconsfield
Bucks HP9 1LG
Tel: 01494 671234
Website: www.nftsfilm-tv.ac.uk
Email: info@nfts.co.uk

ROYAL ACADEMY OF DRAMATIC ART (RADA)
For many the Holy Grail of drama schools, its list of famous past members goes on endlessly (Sir Alan Bates, Ralph Fiennes, Jane Horrocks, Adrian Lester and Joely Richardson). Founded in 1904, it prides itself on its facilities, but mostly on the excellence of its training. As well as its full-time courses it offers short courses and, most importantly for the purposes of this book, a series of youth workshops during the year. These take place on a Saturday and are open to young people aged between 16 and 24. Refer to the website for details or send in a name and address to be included on the mailing list.

62–64 Gower Street
London WC1E 6ED
Tel: 020 7636 7076
Website: www.rada.org

ORGANISATIONS AND GOVERNING BODIES

BRITISH PHONOGRAPHIC INDUSTRY (BPI)
Riverside Building
County Hall
Westminster Bridge Road
London SE1 7JA
Tel: 020 7803 1300
Website: www.bpi.co.uk

BRITISH SOCIETY FOR MUSIC THERAPY (BSMT)
There is a reduced membership rate for full-time students who
wish to become music therapists. Publishes the *BSMT Bulletin*
and the *British Journal of Music Therapy*.

61 Church Hill Road
East Barnet
Herts EN4 8SY
Tel: 020 8441 6226
Website: www.bsmt.org
Email: info@bsmt.org

CONFERENCE OF DRAMA SCHOOLS (CDS)
Founded in 1969, it aims to encourage the highest standards in
training for the theatre, film and TV industries. You can get further
information on CDS member schools and the courses they offer in
the *CDS Guide to Professional Training in Drama and Technical
Theatre*.

The Executive Secretary
PO Box 34252
London NW5 1XJ
Website: www.drama.ac.uk
Email: info@cds.drama.ac.uk

COUNCIL FOR DANCE EDUCATION AND TRAINING (CDET)

The CDET has been set up to promote excellence in dance training provision in this country. It accredits courses at vocational dance schools and gives advice to schools, teachers, students and their parents. It also publishes a wide variety of informative brochures answering the most often asked questions about becoming a dancer including 'An Applicant's Guide to Auditioning and Interviewing at Dance and Drama Schools' and 'A Practical Guide to Vocational Training in Dance and Drama Schools'. For information sheets, send an A4 stamped addressed envelope to:

Old Brewer's Yard
17–19 Neal Street
Covent Garden
London WC2H 9UY
Tel: 020 7240 5703
Website: www.cdet.org.uk
Email: info@cdet.org.uk

DANCE UK

This nationally recognised support agency has been set up by the profession to take action on its behalf. It has a wide range of useful information sheets aimed at professional dancers and dance students including 'Healthier Dancer Programme'. It also has a register of accredited medical and complementary practitioners to treat dancers.

Battersea Arts Centre
Lavender Hill
London SW11 5TF
Tel: 020 7228 4990
Website: www.danceuk.org
Email: info@danceuk.org

EQUITY

The British Actors' Equity Association is the trade union representing performers in arts and entertainment in this country. Its remit not only covers actors but also dancers, stage managers and even singers and directors. You can obtain a leaflet 'How to Join Equity' by writing to the address below; however if you are taking an accredited vocational course in the performing arts Equity offers a student membership, and for those who have completed such a course full Equity membership is automatically given.

Guild House
Upper St Martins Lane
London WC2H 9EG
Tel: 020 7379 6000
Website: www.equity.org.uk
Email: info@equity.co.org.uk

FOUNDATION FOR COMMUNITY DANCE

This national development agency provides information and support about employment and further training opportunities in fields as diverse as youth work, health, disability and the criminal justice system. It also publishes *Network News* fortnightly.

LCB Depot
31 Rutland Street
Leicester LE1 1RE
Tel: 0116 253 3453
Website: www.communitydance.org.uk
Email: info@communitydance.org.uk

INCORPORATED SOCIETY OF MUSICIANS

10 Stratford Place
London W1C 1AA
Tel: 020 7629 4413
Website: www.ism.org
Email: membership@ism.org

MUSICIANS' UNION

The Musician's Union has approximately 31,000 members and strongly defends those members' rights. It offers a variety of services including career advice and discounts on purchasing sheet music, instruments and equipment. It has six regional branches and covers six specialist musical areas: British Music Writers' Council, freelance orchestral, session musicians, folk, roots and traditional music, and jazz and theatre.

60/62 Clapham Road
London SW9 0JJ
Tel: 020 7840 5534
Website: www.musiciansunion.org.uk
Email: info@musiciansunion.org.uk

NATIONAL ASSOCIATION OF YOUTH THEATRES (NAYT)

The NAYT has a comprehensive list of amateur drama clubs and regional youth theatres it can send to you.

Darlington Arts Centre
Vane Terrace
Darlington DL3 7AX
Tel: 01325 363330
Website: www.nayt.org.uk
Email: nayt@btconnect.com

NATIONAL COUNCIL FOR DRAMA TRAINING (NCDT)

The NCDT was set up by the industry to ensure that drama training is of the highest quality and appropriate to the industry's ever-changing needs. It provides general advice and information such as the funding available. You can obtain a list of NCDT accredited courses from the address below.

1–7 Woburn Walk
Bloomsbury
London WC1H 0JJ
Tel: 020 7387 3650
Website: www.ncdt.co.uk
Email: info@ncdt.co.uk

NATIONAL YOUTH THEATRE (NYT)

Scores of ex-members of the NYT have gone on to do great things within the industry. Anyone between 13 and 21 years old (or still attending full-time education) can apply and previous experience is valuable but not essential. Each year more than 3,000 young people are auditioned for NYT courses including Acting, Costume-Making and Lighting and Sound.

443–445 Holloway Road
London N7 6LW
Tel: 020 7281 3863
Website: www.nyt.org.uk

SOCIETY OF TEACHERS OF SPEECH AND DRAMA (STSD)

Behind every good actor is a good drama teacher – from Mrs
Jones who taught them at 11 years old to the professionals giving
them masterclasses at drama school. If you wish to become a
drama teacher, the STSD can give advice and support.

73 Berry Hill Road
Mansfield NG18 4RU
Tel: 01623 627636
Website: www.stsd.org.uk

SPOTLIGHT

Founded in 1927, Spotlight now has over 30,000 members and
provides casting information to the entertainment industry. For
over 75 years its pictures and profiles of actors have helped
casting agents pick the right person for the right job. It now has
an award-winning internet version of Spotlight with a
comprehensive search engine for artist details. It also offers a
dedicated video-casting facility for its members.

7 Leicester Place
London WC2H 7BP
Tel: 020 7437 7631
Website: www.spotlightcd.com

PUBLICATIONS AND PERIODICALS

CONTACTS

The annual directory published by Spotlight and containing
essential information for people working in stage, TV, film and
radio. Entries include a list of agents, dance companies and
organisations, recording studios and theatre companies. Email
info@spotlightcd.com or check the website at www.spotlightcd.com.

CRAC DEGREE COURSE GUIDES 2007/8: MUSIC, DRAMA AND DANCE

Published by Trotman, this gives comparative information on first-degree courses in the performing arts. The book covers the style and content of the courses, teaching and assessment methods, and entrance requirements.

DANCE GAZETTE

Published three times a year by the Royal Academy of Dance, this has articles on dancers, dance companies, choreography, training and teaching.
Website: www.rad.org.uk
Email: gazette@rad.org.uk

DANCE NOW

This quarterly publication covers all aspects of theatrical dance and is aimed at both dance specialists and enthusiasts.
Website: www.dancebooks.co.uk
Email: now@dancebooks.co.uk

DANCE THEATRE JOURNAL

This quarterly magazine covers contemporary dance, ballet and non-western dance and includes interviews with choreographers and dancers.
Website: www.laban.org
Email: dtj@laban.org

DANCING TIMES

Aimed at performers and instructors, this monthly magazine mainly focuses on ballet and contemporary dance.
Website: www.dancing-times.co.uk
Email: dt@dancing-times.co.uk

THE DIRECTORY OF GRANT-MAKING TRUSTS

Published by the Charities Aid Foundation, this lists all the places you can go to find funding for performing arts courses. Your local library should have a copy or contact:

CAF
25 Kings Hill Avenue
Kingshill
West Malling

Kent ME19 4TA
Tel: 01732 520000
Website: www.cafonline.org
Email: enquiries@cafonline.org

MUSIC JOURNAL
The monthly magazine of the Incorporated Society of Musicians
(ISM). Covers news and activities and is read by professional
musicians as well as music students.
Website: www.ism.org
Email: membership@ism.org

MUSIC TEACHER
A monthly magazine aimed at those involved in music education.
Website: www.rhinegold.co.uk
Email: music.teacher@rhinegold.co.uk

MUSIC WEEK
The music industry's weekly bible, covering everything from
finances to new signings, and legal news to distribution.
Website: www.musicweek.com

OPERA
A monthly magazine covering opera events and music worldwide.
Website: www.opera.co.uk
Email: editor@opera.co.uk

OPERA NOW
This bimonthly magazine contains features, live reviews,
interviews and profiles.
Website: www.rhinegold.co.uk
Email: opera.now@rhinegold.co.uk

SCREEN INTERNATIONAL
The film industry's weekly bible. It has everything from news to
statistics and film reviews.
Website: www.screendaily.com

SIGHT AND SOUND

A monthly magazine published by the British Film Institute (BFI) and giving comment, news and features on films both old and new.
Website: www.bfi.org.uk
Email: s&s@bfi.org.uk

THE SINGER

A bimonthly magazine aimed at singers in all aspects of music including classical, jazz, cabaret, choral and musicals.
Website: www.rhinegold.co.uk
Email: the.singer@rhinegold.co.uk

THE STAGE

The actors' weekly bible. It covers everything to do with the entertainment industry including jobs, open audition dates and new openings.
Website: www.thestage.co.uk
Email: gen_enquiries@thestage.co.uk

UNIVERSITY SCHOLARSHIPS, AWARDS AND BURSARIES

Author: Brian Heap. Published by Trotman, this lists scholarships available to students from universities and other organisations.

VARIETY

This weekly newspaper is the American version of *The Stage* – only with more glitz and glamour (as you'd expect as it gives the inside gossip on Hollywood and Broadway). It also publishes reviews of British theatrical shows and gives the top five charts of films, American TV shows and albums. Good to give you a taste of what's actually out there.
Website: www.variety.com

GOVERNMENT AND AWARDING BODIES

CONNEXIONS

Connexions is aimed primarily at 13- to 19-year-olds and gives excellent information on jobs and careers. On the website you will find the 'jobs4u' careers database. This database gives you detailed information on getting into dance, drama and music as

well as having links to related careers in the entertainment and leisure sector including stage manager, drama therapist and arts administrator.
Website: www.connexions-direct.com

CREATIVE AND CULTURAL SKILLS

Creative and Cultural Skills is the Sector Skills Council for advertising, crafts, cultural heritage, design, music, performing, literary and visual arts. It has an excellent database of training courses and if you need advice on funding or on the careers available in this sector you should check out the website.

4th Floor
Lafone House
The Leathermarket
Weston St
London SE1 3HN
Tel: 020 7015 1800
Website: www.ccskills.org.uk
Email: info@ccskills.org.uk

DEPARTMENT FOR EDUCATION AND SKILLS (DfES)

If you are undertaking a vocational training course lasting up to two years (with up to one year's practical work experience if it is part of the course), you may be eligible for a Career Development Loan. These are available for full-time, part-time and distance-learning courses and applicants can be employed, self-employed or unemployed. The DfES pays interest on the loan for the length of the course and up to one month afterwards. You can also obtain information on funding for state-funded higher education courses and on Dance and Drama Awards (DaDAs). The DfES also has a list of Centres of Vocational Excellence in the performing arts around the country.

Information packs available from 0800 585505
Website: www.dfes.gov.uk
www.dfes.gov.uk/cove
or www.surestart.gov.uk

EDEXCEL

Edexcel is now responsible for BTEC qualifications including BTEC First Diplomas, National Diplomas and Higher Nationals (HNC and HND). The website includes qualification quick links. BTEC qualifications in this field include Technical, Performance, Production, Make-up, Musical Theatre, Set Construction, Stage Design, and Circus Skills as well as Acting, Dance, and Music. There have been recent changes to Edexcel so please check the website carefully.

One90 High Holborn
London
WC1V 7BH
Tel: 0870 240 9800
Website: www.edexcel.org.uk

LEARNDIRECT

This free helpline and website can give you impartial information about learning.
Tel: 0800 101 901
Website: www.learndirect.co.uk

LEARNING AND SKILLS COUNCIL

Launched in 2001, Learning and Skills Council (LSC) is responsible for the largest investment in post-16 education and training in England.
Apprenticeship helpline: 0800 015 0600
Website: www.apprenticeships.org.uk

In Scotland:
Website: www.modernapprenticeships.com
or www.careers.scotland.org.uk

In Wales:
www.beskilled.net

SKILLSEEKERS

Run by local enterprise companies in Scotland, Skillseekers is a training programme for young people aged 16–24. It encourages employers to train young people towards a recognised workplace qualification by helping them with the cost of training. The scheme is open to people who have left school and have a job or are looking for work.

For more information, contact your local Careers Scotland Centre (ring 0845 850 2502 to find your nearest one) or look on the Scottish Enterprise website: www.scottish-enterprise.com.

SKILLSET

Skillset is the industry organisation set up to look after training for the independent and freelance sectors of the film, TV, video and radio industries. It collects information on existing training provision and promotes adequate training for new entrants.

Prospect House
80–110 New Oxford Street
London WC1A 1HB
Tel: 020 7520 5757
Website: www.skillset.org
Email: info@skillset.org